THE FLOWERS OF EVIL

CHARLES BAUDELAIRE

Born in Paris, April 9, 1821

1832-35 boarding student at the College Royale, Lyons

1836-39 student at the Lycée Louis-le-Grand, Paris

1841-42 (June-Feb.) sea voyage around the Cape of Good Hope as far as Mauritius and Réunion. Returned to Paris

1856 — *Les Histoires Extraordinaires,* the first of Baudelaire's Poe translations appeared in book form

1857 — June 25, publication of the first edition of *Les Fleurs du Mal*

1857 — August, trial for obscenity against *Les Fleurs du Mal,* resulted in the banning of six poems

1861 — The last of Baudelaire's great articles on art, this one inspired by the death of Delacroix

1864 — Left Paris in April to undertake a lecture tour in Belgium

1866 — July, brought back from Belgium, stricken with paralysis

Died in Paris, August 31, 1867

CHARLES BAUDELAIRE

THE
FLOWERS OF EVIL

A SELECTION EDITED BY

Marthiel and Jackson Mathews

A NEW DIRECTIONS PAPERBOOK

Library of Congress Catalog Card No. 58-9276
First published as New Directions Paperbook No. 71
(ISBN: 0-8112-0006-x), 1958

ACKNOWLEDGMENTS

*For permission to reprint the copyright translations in this volume,
the editors and publisher are indebted to the following translators,
their heirs and publishers:*

Brandt & Brandt for translations by George Dillon and Edna St.
    Vincent Millay from *Flowers of Evil*, translated from the French
    of Charles Baudelaire, published by Harper & Brothers, Copy-
    right 1936 by George Dillon and Edna St. Vincent Millay
Thomas Cole, editor and publisher of *Imagi*, for the translation
    "Invitation to the Voyage" by Richard Wilbur
Harper & Brothers for "Lesbians" from *The Cicadas and Other
    Poems*, Copyright 1929, 1931 by Aldous Huxley
Pantheon Books, Inc. for translations by Roy Campbell from *Poems
    of Baudelaire*, Copyright 1952 by Pantheon Books, Inc.
The Richards Press Ltd. for translations by James Elroy Flecker
Random House, Inc. for the translation "The Giantess" by Karl
    Shapiro from *Person, Place and Thing*, Copyright 1942 by
    Karl Shapiro
Allan Swallow, publisher, for "The Skeleton Laborer" from *Col-
    lected Poems* by Yvor Winters, Copyright 1952 by Yvor Winters
Miss Ann Wolfe for "The Gaming Table" by Humbert Wolfe

Barbara Gibbs   Dorothy Martin   Graham Reynolds
Kenneth O. Hanson   David Paul   Sir John Squire

Manufactured in the United States of America
New Directions books are printed on acid-free paper.
Published simultaneously in Canada by Penguin Books Canada Limited

New Directions Books are published for James Laughlin
by New Directions Publishing Corporation,
80 Eighth Avenue, New York 10011.

TWENTY-SECOND PRINTING

FOREWORD

Baudelaire is one of that small company of poets who with a single book of short poems have permanently affected the history and nature of poetry. The *Flowers of Evil* have now passed their first century. They have been translated into all the principal languages of the world.

From the one hundred and sixty-three poems of the complete bilingual edition (New Directions 1955), we have here chosen fifty-three of the finest translations. Several poems which we should have liked to include, for themselves, have been omitted as less effective in the English version. "The Skeleton Laborer" by Yvor Winters (p. 95) did not appear in our former collection.

Baudelaire over a period of several years made notes and drafts for a preface, which he planned for the second (1861) and again for the third (1868) edition of his poems, but which he left unfinished, probably on the advice of his publisher. These form "Three Drafts of a Preface," which first appeared in English in our edition of 1955; the translation is based on the text given in the critical edition of *Les Fleurs du Mal* by Jacques Crépet and Georges Blin.

The texts of the poems are those established by Yves Gérard Le Dantec for the Pléiade edition.

CONTENTS

ix

CONTENTS

THREE DRAFTS OF A PREFACE

by Charles Baudelaire

I

PREFACE

France is passing through a period of vulgarity. Paris, a center radiating universal stupidity. Despite Molière and Béranger, no one would ever have believed that France would take to the road of progress at such a rate. Matters of art, *terrae incognitae*.

Great men are stupid.

My book may have done some good; I do not regret that. It may have done harm; I do not rejoice at that.

The aim of poetry. This book is not made for my wives, my daughters, or my sisters.

Every sin, every crime I have related has been imputed to me.

Hatred and contempt as forms of amusement. Elegists are vulgar scum. *Et verbum caro factum est.* The poet is of no party. Otherwise, he would be a mere mortal.

The Devil. Original sin. Man as good. If you would, you could be the Tyrant's favorite; it is more difficult to love God than to believe in Him. On the other hand, it is more difficult for people nowadays to believe in the Devil than to love him. Everyone smells him and no one believes in him. Sublime subtlety of the Devil.

A soul to my liking. The scene. — Thus, novelty. — The Epigraph. — D'Aurevilly. — The Renaissance. — Gérard de Nerval. — We are all hanged or hangable.

I have included a certain amount of filth to please the gentlemen of the press. They have proved ungrateful.

II

PREFACE TO THE FLOWERS

It is not for my wives, my daughters, or my sisters that this book has been written; nor for the wives, daughters, or sisters of my neighbors. I leave that to those who have some reason to confuse good deeds with fine language.

I know the passionate lover of fine style exposes himself to the hatred of the masses; but no respect for humanity, no false modesty, no conspiracy, no universal suffrage will ever force me to speak the unspeakable jargon of this age, or to confuse ink with virtue.

Certain illustrious poets have long since divided among themselves the more flowery provinces of the realm of poetry. I have found it amusing, and the more pleasant because the task was more difficult, to extract *beauty* from *Evil*. This book, which is quintessentially useless and absolutely innocent, was written with no other aim than to divert myself and to practice my passionate taste for the difficult.

Some have told me that these poems might do harm; I have not rejoiced at that. Others, good souls, that they might do good; and that has given me no regret. I was equally surprised at the former's fear and the latter's hope, which only served to prove once again that this age has unlearned all the classical notions of literature.

Despite the encouragement a few celebrated pedants have given to man's natural stupidity, I should never have believed our country could move with such speed along the road of *progress*. The world has taken on a thickness of vulgarity that raises a spiritual man's contempt to the violence of a passion. But there are those happy hides so thick that poison itself could not penetrate them.

I had intended, at first, to answer numerous criticisms and at the same time to explain a few quite simple questions that have been totally obscured by modern enlightenment: What is poetry? What is its aim? On the distinction between the Good and the Beautiful; on the Beauty in Evil; that rhythm and rhyme answer the immortal need in man for monotony, symmetry, and surprise; on adapting style to subject; on the vanity and danger of inspiration, etc., etc.; but this morning I was so rash as to read some of the public newspapers; suddenly an indolence of the weight of twenty atmospheres fell upon me, and I was stopped, faced by the appalling uselessness of explaining anything whatever to anyone whatever. Those who know can divine me, and for those who can not or will not understand, it would be fruitless to pile up explanations.

C.B.

How the artist, by a prescribed series of exercises, can proportionately increase his originality;

How poetry is related to music through prosody, whose roots go deeper into the human soul than any classical theory indicates;

That French poetry possesses a mysterious and unrecognized prosody, like the Latin and English languages;

Why any poet who does not know exactly how many rhymes each word has is incapable of expressing any idea whatever;

That the poetic phrase can imitate (and in this, it is like the art of music and the science of mathematics) a horizontal line, an ascending or descending vertical line; that it can rise straight up to heaven without losing its breath, or go perpendicularly to hell with the velocity of any weight; that it can follow a spiral, describe a parabola, or zigzag, making a series of superimposed angles;

xiii

That poetry is like the arts of painting, cooking, and cosmetics in its ability to express every sensation of sweetness or bitterness, beatitude or horror, by coupling a certain noun with a certain adjective, in analogy or contrast;

How, by relying on my principles and using the knowledge which I guarantee to teach him in twenty lessons, any man can learn to compose a tragedy that will be no more hooted at than another, or line up a poem long enough to be as dull as any epic known.

A difficult matter, to rise to that divine callousness! For, despite my most commendable efforts, even I have not been able to resist the desire to please my contemporaries, as witness in several places, laid on like make-up, certain patches of base flattery aimed at democracy, and even a certain amount of filth meant to excuse the dreariness of my subject. But the gentlemen of the press having proved ungrateful for tender attentions of this kind, I have eliminated every trace of both, so far as possible, from this new edition.

I propose, in order to prove again the excellence of my method, to apply it in the near future to celebrating the pleasures of devotion and the raptures of military glory, though I have never known either.

Notes on plagiarisms. — Thomas Gray. Edgar Poe (2 passages). Longfellow (2 passages). Statius. Virgil (the whole of Andromache). Aeschylus. Victor Hugo.

III

DRAFT OF A PREFACE FOR THE *Flowers of Evil*

(*To be combined perhaps with earlier notes*)

If there is any glory in not being understood, or in being only very slightly so, I may without boasting say that with this little book I have at a single stroke both won and deserved that glory. Submitted several times over to various publishers who rejected it with disgust, put on trial and mutilated in 1857 as a result of a quite bizarre misapprehension, then gradually revived, augmented, and fortified during several years' silence, only to disappear again thanks to my losing interest, this discordant product of the *Muse of modern times,* again enlivened with a few violent new touches, dares today for the third time to face the sun of stupidity.

This is not my fault, but that of an insistent publisher who thinks he is strong enough to brave the public distaste. "This book will remain a stain on your whole life," one of my friends, a great poet, predicted from the beginning. And indeed all my misadventures have so far justified him. But I have one of those happy characters that enjoy hatred and feel glorified by contempt. My diabolically passionate taste for stupidity makes me take peculiar pleasure in the falsifications of calumny. Being as chaste as paper, as sober as water, as devout as a woman at communion, as harmless as a sacrificial lamb, it would not displease me to be taken for a debauchee, a drunkard, an infidel, a murderer. My publisher insists that it might be of some use, to me and to him, to explain why and how I have written this book, what were my means and aim, my plan and method. Such a critical task might well have the luck to interest those minds that love profound rhetoric. For those I shall perhaps write it later on and have it printed in ten copies. But, on second thought, doesn't it seem obvious that this would be a quite superfluous undertaking for everyone concerned since those are the minds that already know or guess and the rest will never understand? I have too much fear of being ridiculous to wish to breathe into the mass of humanity the understanding of an art object; in doing so, I should fear to resemble those

Utopians who by decree wish to make all Frenchmen rich and virtuous at a single stroke. And moreover, my best, my supreme reason is that it annoys and bores me. Do we invite the crowd, the audience, behind the scenes, into the workshops of the costume and scene designers; into the actress's dressing-room? Do we show the public (enthusiastic today, tomorrow indifferent) the mechanism behind our effects? Do we explain to them the revisions, the improvisations adopted in rehearsal, and even to what extent instinct and sincerity are mixed with artifice and charlatanry, all indispensable to the amalgam that is the work itself? Do we display all the rags, the rouge, the pulleys, the chains, the alterations, the scribbled-over proof sheets, in short all the horrors that make up the sanctuary of art?

In any case, such is not my mood today. I have no desire either to demonstrate, to astonish, to amuse, or to persuade. I have my nerves and my vertigo. I aspire to absolute rest and continuous night. Though I have sung the mad pleasures of wine and opium, I thirst only for a liquor unknown on earth, which the pharmaceutics of heaven itself could not afford me; a liquor that contains neither vitality nor death, neither excitation nor extinction. To know nothing, to teach nothing, to will nothing, to feel nothing, to sleep and still to sleep, this today is my only wish. A base and loathsome wish, but sincere.

Nevertheless, since the best of taste teaches us not to fear contradicting ourselves a bit, I have collected at the end of this abominable book certain testimonials of sympathy from a few of the men I prize most, so that an impartial reader may infer from them that I am not absolutely deserving of excommunication, and that since I have managed to make myself loved of some, my heart, whatever a certain printed rag may have said of it, is perhaps not "as frightfully hideous as my face."

Finally, the uncommon generosity which those gentlemen, the critics . . .

Since ignorance is increasing . . .

I take it on myself to denounce imitations . . .

(Translated by J.M.)

THE FLOWERS OF EVIL

AU LECTEUR

La sottise, l'erreur, le péché, la lésine,
Occupent nos esprits et travaillent nos corps,
Et nous alimentons nos aimables remords,
Comme les mendiants nourrissent leur vermine.

Nos péchés sont têtus, nos repentirs sont lâches;
Nous nous faisons payer grassement nos aveux,
Et nous rentrons gaiement dans le chemin bourbeux,
Croyant par de vils pleurs laver toutes nos taches.

Sur l'oreiller du mal c'est Satan Trismégiste
Qui berce longuement notre esprit enchanté,
Et le riche métal de notre volonté
Est tout vaporisé par ce savant chimiste.

C'est le Diable qui tient les fils qui nous remuent !
Aux objets répugnants nous trouvons des appas;
Chaque jour vers l'Enfer nous descendons d'un pas,
Sans horreur, à travers des ténèbres qui puent.

Ainsi qu'un débauché pauvre qui baise et mange
Le sein martyrisé d'une antique catin,
Nous volons au passage un plaisir clandestin
Que nous pressons bien fort comme une vieille orange.

Serré, fourmillant, comme un million d'helminthes,
Dans nos cerveaux ribote un peuple de Démons,
Et, quand nous respirons, la Mort dans nos poumons
Descend, fleuve invisible, avec de sourdes plaintes.

TO THE READER

Folly and error, avarice and vice,
Employ our souls and waste our bodies' force.
As mangy beggars incubate their lice,
We nourish our innocuous remorse.

Our sins are stubborn, craven our repentance.
For our weak vows we ask excessive prices.
Trusting our tears will wash away the sentence,
We sneak off where the muddy road entices.

Cradled in evil, that Thrice-Great Magician,
The Devil, rocks our souls, that can't resist;
And the rich metal of our own volition
Is vaporized by that sage alchemist.

The Devil pulls the strings by which we're worked :
By all revolting objects lured, we slink
Hellwards; each day down one more step we're jerked
Feeling no horror, through the shades that stink.

Just as a lustful pauper bites and kisses
The scarred and shrivelled breast of an old whore,
We steal, along the roadside, furtive blisses,
Squeezing them like stale oranges for more.

Packed tight, like hives of maggots, thickly seething,
Within our brains a host of demons surges.
Deep down into our lungs at every breathing,
Death flows, an unseen river, moaning dirges.

3

Si le viol, le poison, le poignard, l'incendie,
N'ont pas encor brodé de leurs plaisants dessins
Le canevas banal de nos piteux destins,
C'est que notre âme, hélas ! n'est pas assez hardie.

Mais parmi les chacals, les panthères, les lices,
Les singes, les scorpions, les vautours, les serpents,
Les monstres glapissants, hurlants, grognants, rampants,
Dans la ménagerie infâme de nos vices,

Il en est un plus laid, plus méchant, plus immonde !
Quoiqu'il ne pousse ni grands gestes ni grands cris,
Il ferait volontiers de la terre un débris
Et dans un bâillement avalerait le monde;

C'est l'Ennui ! — l'œil chargé d'un pleur involontaire,
Il rêve d'échafauds en fumant son houka.
Tu le connais, lecteur, ce monstre délicat,
— Hypocrite lecteur, — mon semblable, — mon frère !

BÉNÉDICTION

Lorsque, par un décret des puissances suprêmes,
Le Poëte apparaît en ce monde ennuyé,
Sa mère épouvantée et pleine de blasphèmes
Crispe ses poings vers Dieu, qui la prend en pitié :

— " Ah ! que n'ai-je mis bas tout un nœud de vipères,
Plutôt que de nourrir cette dérision !

If rape or arson, poison, or the knife
Has wove no pleasing patterns in the stuff
Of this drab canvas we accept as life —
It is because we are not bold enough !

Amongst the jackals, leopards, mongrels, apes,
Snakes, scorpions, vultures, that with hellish din,
Squeal, roar, writhe, gambol, crawl, with monstrous shapes,
In each man's foul menagerie of sin —

There's one more damned than all. He never gambols,
Nor crawls, nor roars, but, from the rest withdrawn,
Gladly of this whole earth would make a shambles
And swallow up existence with a yawn . . .

Boredom ! He smokes his hookah, while he dreams
Of gibbets, weeping tears he cannot smother.
You know this dainty monster, too, it seems —
Hypocrite reader ! — You ! — My twin ! — My brother !

—Roy Campbell

THE BLESSING

When, by a decree of the sovereign power,
The poet makes his appearance in a bored world,
With fists clenched at the horror, his outraged mother
Calls on a pitying God, at whom these curses are hurled :

" Why was I not made to litter a brood of vipers
Rather than conceive this human mockery ?

5

Maudite soit la nuit aux plaisirs éphémères
Où mon ventre a conçu mon expiation !

Puisque tu m'as choisie entre toutes les femmes
Pour être le dégoût de mon triste mari,
Et que je ne puis pas rejeter dans les flammes,
Comme un billet d'amour, ce monstre rabougri,

Je ferai rejaillir ta haine qui m'accable
Sur l'instrument maudit de tes méchancetés,
Et je tordrai si bien cet arbre misérable,
Qu'il ne pourra pousser ses boutons empestés ! "

Elle ravale ainsi l'écume de sa haine,
Et, ne comprenant pas les desseins éternels,
Elle-même prépare au fond de la Géhenne
Les bûchers consacrés aux crimes maternels.

Pourtant, sous la tutelle invisible d'un Ange,
L'Enfant déshérité s'enivre de soleil,
Et dans tout ce qu'il boit et dans tout ce qu'il mange
Retrouve l'ambroisie et le nectar vermeil.

Il joue avec le vent, cause avec le nuage,
Et s'enivre en chantant du chemin de la croix;
Et l'Esprit qui le suit dans son pèlerinage
Pleure de le voir gai comme un oiseau des bois.

Tous ceux qu'il veut aimer l'observent avec crainte,
Ou bien, s'enhardissant de sa tranquillité,
Cherchent à qui saura lui tirer une plainte,
Et font sur lui l'essai de leur férocité.

My curses on that night whose ephemeral pleasures
Filled my womb with this avenging treachery !

Since I must be chosen among all women that are
To bear the lifetime's grudge of a sullen husband,
And since I cannot get rid of this caricature,
— Fling it away like old letters to be burned,

On what you have devised for my punishment
I will let all your hate of me rebound,
I will torture this stunted growth until its bent
Branches let fall every blighted bud to the ground ! "

And so she prepares for herself in Hell's pit
A place on the pyre made for a mother's crimes,
Blind, in the fury of her foaming hatred,
To the meaning and purpose of the eternal designs.

Meanwhile, under the care of an unseen angel,
The disinherited Child revels in the sun's
Bright force; all that he eats and drinks can fill
Him with memories of the food that was heaven's.

The wind his plaything, any cloud a friend,
The Spirit watching can only weep to see
How in childhood his way of the cross is lightened
With the wild bird-song of his innocent gaiety.

Those he would love look at him with suspicion
Or else, emboldened by his calm, experiment
With various possible methods of exciting derision
By trying out their cruelty on his complaint.

7

Dans le pain et le vin destinés à sa bouche
Ils mêlent de la cendre avec d'impurs crachats;
Avec hypocrisie ils jettent ce qu'il touche,
Et s'accusent d'avoir mis leurs pieds dans ses pas.

Sa femme va criant sur les places publiques :
" Puisqu'il me trouve assez belle pour m'adorer,
Je ferai le métier des idoles antiques,
Et comme elles je veux me faire redorer;

Et je me soûlerai de nard, d'encens, de myrrhe,
De génuflexions, de viandes et de vins,
Pour savoir si je puis dans un cœur qui m'admire
Usurper en riant les hommages divins !

Et, quand je m'ennuierai de ces farces impies,
Je poserai sur lui ma frêle et forte main;
Et mes ongles, pareils aux ongles des harpies,
Sauront jusqu'à son cœur se frayer un chemin.

Comme un tout jeune oiseau qui tremble et qui pal-
J'arracherai ce cœur tout rouge de son sein,   [pite,
Et, pour rassasier ma bête favorite,
Je le lui jetterai par terre avec dédain ! "

Vers le Ciel, où son œil voit un trône splendide,
Le Poëte serein lève ses bras pieux,
Et les vastes éclairs de son esprit lucide
Lui dérobent l'aspect des peuples furieux :

— " Soyez béni, mon Dieu, qui donnez la souffrance
Comme un divin remède à nos impuretés

They mix ashes or unspeakable filth with the bread
And the wine of his daily communion, drop
Whatever he may have touched with affected dread,
And studiously avoid wherever he may step.

His mistress, parading her contempt in the street,
Cries : " Since he finds my beauty a thing to worship,
I will be one of the ancient idols he talks about,
And make myself with gold out of the same workshop!

I will never have enough of his kneelings and offerings
Until I am sure that the choice foods, the wines,
The ' nard,' the ' incense,' the ' myrrh ' that he brings
He brings as other men would to the Virgin's shrines.

And when I am sick to death of trying not to laugh
At the farce of my black masses, I'll try the force
Of the hand he calls ' frail,' my nails will dig a path
Like harpies', to the heart that beats for me, of course !

Like a nestling trembling and palpitating
I will pull that red heart out of his breast
And throw it down for my favourite dog's eating
— Let him do whatever he likes with the rest ! "

A serene piety, lifting the poet's gaze,
Reveals heaven opening on a shining throne,
And the lower vision of the world's ravening rage
Is shut off by the sheet lightnings of his brain.

" Be blessed, oh my God, who givest suffering
As the only divine remedy for our folly,

9

Et comme la meilleure et la plus pure essence
Qui prépare les forts aux saintes voluptés !

Je sais que vous gardez une place au Poëte
Dans les rangs bienheureux des saintes Légions,
Et que vous l'invitez à l'éternelle fête
Des Trônes, des Vertus, des Dominations.

Je sais que la douleur est la noblesse unique
Où ne mordront jamais la terre et les enfers,
Et qu'il faut pour tresser ma couronne mystique
Imposer tous les temps et tous les univers.

Mais les bijoux perdus de l'antique Palmyre,
Les métaux inconnus, les perles de la mer,
Par votre main montés, ne pourraient pas suffire
A ce beau diadème éblouissant et clair;

Car il ne sera fait que de pure lumière,
Puisée au foyer saint des rayons primitifs,
Et dont les yeux mortels, dans leur splendeur entière,
Ne sont que des miroirs obscurcis et plaintifs ! "

LES PHARES

Rubens, fleuve d'oubli, jardin de la paresse,
Oreiller de chair fraîche où l'on ne peut aimer,
Mais où la vie afflue et s'agite sans cesse,
Comme l'air dans le ciel et la mer dans la mer;

As the highest and purest essence preparing
The strong in spirit for ecstasies most holy.

I know that among the uplifted legions
Of saints, a place awaits the Poet's arrival,
And that among the Powers, Virtues, Dominations
He too is summoned to Heaven's festival.

I know that sorrow is the one human strength
On which neither earth nor hell can impose,
And that all the universe and all time's length
Must be wound into the mystic crown for my brows.

But all the treasury of buried Palmyra,
The earth's unknown metals, the sea's pearls,
Mounted by Thy hand, would be deemed an inferior
Glitter, to his diadem that shines without jewels.

For Thou knowest it will be made of purest light
Drawn from the holy hearth of every primal ray,
To which all human eyes, if they were one bright
Eye, are only a tarnished mirror's fading day!"

—David Paul

BEACONS

Rubens, garden of idleness watered by oblivion,
Where quick flesh pillows the impotence of dreams,
Where life's affluence writhes in eddying abandon
Like air in the air, or water in streams.

II

Léonard de Vinci, miroir profond et sombre,
Où des anges charmants, avec un doux souris
Tout chargé de mystère, apparaissent à l'ombre
Des glaciers et des pins qui ferment leur pays;

Rembrandt, triste hôpital tout rempli de murmures,
Et d'un grand crucifix décoré seulement,
Où la prière en pleurs s'exhale des ordures,
Et d'un rayon d'hiver traversé brusquement;

Michel-Ange, lieu vague où l'on voit des Hercules
Se mêler à des Christs, et se lever tout droits
Des fantômes puissants qui dans les crépuscules
Déchirent leur suaire en étirant leurs doigts;

Colères de boxeur, impudences de faune,
Toi qui sus ramasser la beauté des goujats,
Grand cœur gonflé d'orgueil, homme débile et jaune,
Puget, mélancolique empereur des forçats;

Watteau, ce carnaval où bien des cœurs illustres,
Comme des papillons, errent en flamboyant,
Décors frais et légers éclairés par des lustres
Qui versent la folie à ce bal tournoyant;

Goya, cauchemar plein de choses inconnues,
De fœtus qu'on fait cuire au milieu des sabbats,
De vieilles au miroir et d'enfants toutes nues,
Pour tenter les démons ajustant bien leurs bas;

Delacroix, lac de sang hanté des mauvais anges,
Ombragé par un bois de sapins toujours vert,

12

Leonardo da Vinci, deep mirror of darkness,
Where angels appear, their smiles charged with mystery
And tenderness, within the shadowy enclosures
Of pines and glaciers that shut in their country.

Rembrandt, tragic hospital re-echoing round a sigh;
A tall crucifix for only ornament
Traversed obliquely by a single wintry ray
Through which prayers rise, exhaling from excrement.

Michelangelo, no man's land where Hercules and Christ
Are at one; where powerful phantoms in crowds
Erect themselves deliberately in darkening twilights,
With pressed, rigid fingers ripping open their shrouds.

Rage of the wrestler, impudence of the faun;
Puget, the convicts' melancholy emperor,
Caging the lion's pride in a weak, jaundiced man,
Deducing beauty from crime, vice and terror.

Watteau, carnival where many a distinguished soul
Flutters like a moth, lost in the brilliance
Of chandeliers shedding frivolity on the cool,
Clear decors enclosing the changes of the dance.

Goya, nightmare compact of things incredible :
Foetuses being fried for a witch's sabbath feast;
An old woman at a mirror, a little naked girl
Lowering an artful stocking to tempt a devil's lust.

Delacroix, blood lake haunted by evil angels
In the permanent green darkness of a forest of firs,

Où, sous un ciel chagrin, des fanfares étranges
Passent, comme un soupir étouffé de Weber;

Ces malédictions, ces blasphèmes, ces plaintes,
Ces extases, ces cris, ces pleurs, ces *Te Deum,*
Sont un écho redit par mille labyrinthes;
C'est pour les cœurs mortels un divin opium !

C'est un cri répété par mille sentinelles,
Un ordre renvoyé par mille porte-voix;
C'est un phare allume sur mille citadelles,
Un appel de chasseurs perdus dans les grands bois !

Car c'est vraiment, Seigneur, le meilleur témoignage
Que nous puissions donner de notre dignité
Que cet ardent sanglot qui roule d'âge en âge
Et vient mourir au bord de votre éternité !

LA VIE ANTÉRIEURE

J'ai longtemps habité sous de vastes portiques
Que les soleils marins teignaient de mille feux,
Et que leurs grands piliers, droits et majestueux,
Rendaient pareils, le soir, aux grottes basaltiques.

Les houles, en roulant les images des cieux,
Mêlaient d'une façon solennelle et mystique
Les tout-puissants accords de leur riche musique
Aux couleurs du couchant reflété par mes yeux.

Where under a stricken sky a muffled sigh fills
The air like a faintly echoed fanfare of Weber's.

Such, O Lord, are the maledictions, the tears,
The ecstasies, the blasphemies, the cries of Te Deum
Re-echoing along labyrinthine corridors :
A dream for mortal hearts distilled from divine opium,

The watchword reiterated by sentinels
A thousand times, the message whispered from post to post,
A beacon burning on a thousand citadels,
A call of all the hunters lost in the great forest.

For is this not indeed, O Lord, the best witness
That our dignity can render to Your pity,
This tide of tears which age after age gathers
To fail and fall on the shore of Your eternity ?

—David Paul

A FORMER LIFE

Long since, I lived beneath vast porticoes,
By many ocean-sunsets tinged and fired,
Where mighty pillars, in majestic rows,
Seemed like basaltic caves when day expired.

The rolling surge that mirrored all the skies
Mingled its music, turbulent and rich,
Solemn and mystic, with the colours which
The setting sun reflected in my eyes.

15

C'est là que j'ai vécu dans les voluptés calmes,
Au milieu de l'azur, des vagues, des splendeurs
Et des esclaves nus, tout imprégnés d'odeurs,

Qui me rafraîchissaient le front avec des palmes,
Et dont l'unique soin était d'approfondir
Le secret douloureux qui me faisait languir.

DON JUAN AUX ENFERS

Quand don Juan descendit vers l'onde souterraine
Et lorsqu'il eut donné son obole à Charon,
Un sombre mendiant, l'œil fier comme Antisthène,
D'un bras vengeur et fort saisit chaque aviron.

Montrant leurs seins pendants et leurs robes ouvertes,
Des femmes se tordaient sous le noir firmament,
Et, comme un grand troupeau de victimes offertes,
Derrière lui traînaient un long mugissement.

Sganarelle en riant lui réclamait ses gages,
Tandis que Don Luis avec un doigt tremblant
Montrait à tous les morts errant sur les rivages
Le fils audacieux qui railla son front blanc.

Frissonnant sous son deuil, la chaste et maigre Elvire,
Près de l'époux perfide et qui fut son amant,
Semblait lui réclamer un suprême sourire
Où brillât la douceur de son premier serment.

And there I lived amid voluptuous calms,
In splendours of blue sky and wandering wave,
Tended by many a naked, perfumed slave,

Who fanned my languid brow with waving palms.
They were my slaves — the only care they had
To know what secret grief had made me sad.

—F. P. Sturm

DON JUAN IN HELL

The night Don Juan came to pay his fees
To Charon, by the caverned water's shore,
A Beggar, proud-eyed as Antisthenes,
Stretched out his knotted fingers on the oar.

Mournful, with drooping breasts and robes unsewn
The shapes of women swayed in ebon skies,
Trailing behind him with a restless moan
Like cattle herded for a sacrifice.

Here, grinning for his wage, stood Sganarelle,
And here Don Luis pointed, bent and dim,
To show the dead who lined the holes of Hell,
This was that impious son who mocked at him.

The hollow-eyed, the chaste Elvira came,
Trembling and veiled, to view her traitor spouse.
Was it one last bright smile she thought to claim,
Such as made sweet the morning of his vows ?

17

Tout droit dans son armure, un grand homme de pierre
Se tenait à la barre et coupait le flot noir;
Mais le calme héros, courbé sur sa rapière,
Regardait le sillage et ne daignait rien voir.

CHATIMENT DE L'ORGUEIL

En ces temps merveilleux où la Théologie
Fleurit avec le plus de séve et d'énergie,
On raconte qu'un jour un docteur des plus grands,
— Après avoir forcé les cœurs indifférents;
Les avoir remués dans leurs profondeurs noires;
Après avoir franchi vers les célestes gloires
Des chemins singuliers à lui-même inconnus,
Où les purs Esprits seuls peut-être étaient venus, —
Comme un homme monté trop haut, pris de panique,
S'écria, transporté d'un orgueil satanique :
" Jésus, petit Jésus ! Je t'ai poussé bien haut !
Mais, si j'avais voulu t'attaquer au défaut
De l'armure, ta honte égalerait ta gloire,
Et tu ne serais plus qu'un fœtus dérisoire ! "

Immédiatement sa raison s'en alla.
L'éclat de ce soleil d'un crêpe se voila;
Tout le chaos roula dans cette intelligence,
Temple autrefois vivant, plein d'ordre et d'opulence,
Sous les plafonds duquel tant de pompe avait lui.
Le silence et la nuit s'installèrent en lui,
Comme dans un caveau dont la clef est perdue.

A great stone man rose like a tower on board,
Stood at the helm and cleft the flood profound :
But the calm hero, leaning on his sword,
Gazed back, and would not offer one look round.

—James Elroy Flecker

THE PUNISHMENT OF PRIDE

In those old times wherein Theology
Flourished with greater sap and energy,
A celebrated doctor — so they say —
Having stirred many careless hearts one day
Down to their dullest depths, and having shown
Strange pathways leading to the heavenly throne —
Tracks he himself had never journeyed on
(Whereby maybe pure spirits alone had gone) —
Frenzied and swollen by a devilish pride,
Like to a man who has climbed too high, outcried :
" Ah, little Jesus, I have lifted thee !
But had I willed to assault thy dignity,
Thy shame had matched thy present fame, and lo !
Thou wouldst be but a wretched embryo ! "

Straightway his reason left him; that keen mind,
Sunbright before, was darkened and made blind;
All chaos whirled within that intellect
Erewhile a shrine with all fair gems bedeckt,
Beneath whose roof such pomp had shone so bright;
He was possessed by silence and thick night
As is a cellar when its key is lost . . .

19

Dès lors il fut semblable aux bêtes de la rue,
Et, quand il s'en allait sans rien voir, à travers
Les champs, sans distinguer les étés des hivers,
Sale, inutile et laid comme une chose usée,
Il faisait des enfants la joie et la risée.

LA GÉANTE

Du temps que la Nature en sa verve puissante
Concevait chaque jour des enfants monstrueux,
J'eusse aimé vivre auprès d'une jeune géante,
Comme aux pieds d'une reine un chat voluptueux.

J'eusse aimé voir son corps fleurir avec son âme
Et grandir librement dans ses terribles jeux;
Deviner si son cœur couve une sombre flamme
Aux humides brouillards qui nagent dans ses yeux;

Parcourir à loisir ses magnifiques formes;
Ramper sur le versant de ses genoux énormes,
Et parfois en été, quand les soleils malsains,

Lasse, la font s'étendre à travers la campagne,
Dormir nonchalamment à l'ombre de ses seins,
Comme un hameau paisible au pied d'une montagne.

Thenceforth he was a brute beast; when he crossed
The fields at times, not seeing any thing,
Knowing not if it were winter or green spring,
Useless, repulsive, vile, he made a mock
For infants, a mere children's laughing-stock.

— Sir John Squire

GIANTESS

When Nature once in lustful hot undress
Conceived gargantuan offspring, then would I
Have loved to live near a young giantess,
Like a voluptuous cat at a queen's feet.

To see her body flower with her desire
And freely spread out in its dreadful play,
Guess if her heart concealed some heavy fire
Whose humid smokes would swim upon her eye.

To feel at leisure her stupendous shapes,
Crawl on the cliffs of her enormous knees,
And, when in summer the unhealthy suns

Have stretched her out across the plains, fatigued,
Sleep in the shadows of her breasts at ease
Like a small hamlet at a mountain's base.

— Karl Shapiro

21

LES BIJOUX

La très-chère était nue, et, connaissant mon cœur,
Elle n'avait gardé que ses bijoux sonores,
Dont le riche attirail lui donnait l'air vainqueur
Qu'ont dans leurs jours heureux les esclaves des Mores.

Quand il jette en dansant son bruit vif et moqueur,
Ce monde rayonnant de métal et de pierre
Me ravit en extase, et j'aime à la fureur
Les choses où le son se mêle à la lumière.

Elle était donc couchée et se laissait aimer,
Et du haut du divan elle souriait d'aise
A mon amour profond et doux comme la mer,
Qui vers elle montait comme vers sa falaise.

Les yeux fixés sur moi, comme un tigre dompté,
D'un air vague et rêveur elle essayait des poses,
Et la candeur unie à la lubricité
Donnait un charme neuf à ses métamorphoses;

Et son bras et sa jambe, et sa cuisse et ses reins,
Polis comme de l'huile, onduleux comme un cygne,
Passaient devant mes yeux clairvoyants et sereins;
Et son ventre et ses seins, ces grappes de ma vigne,

S'avançaient, plus câlins que les Anges du mal,
Pour troubler le repos où mon âme était mise,
Et pour la déranger du rocher de cristal
Où, calme et solitaire, elle s'était assise.

JEWELS

The darling one was naked and, knowing my wish,
Had kept only the regalia of her jewelry
Whose resonant charms can lure and vanquish
Like a Moorish slave-girl's in her moment of glory.

A world of dazzling stones and of precious metals
Flinging, in its quick rhythm, glints of mockery
Ravishes me into ecstasy, I love to madness
The mingling of sounds and lights in one intricacy.

Naked, then, she was to all of my worship,
Smiling in triumph from the heights of her couch
At my desire advancing, as gentle and deep
As the sea sending its waves to the warm beach.

Her eyes fixed as a tiger's in the tamer's trance,
Absent, unthinking, she varied her poses
With an audacity and wild innocence
That gave a strange pang to each metamorphosis.

Her long legs, her hips, shining smooth as oil,
Her arms and her thighs, undulant as a swan,
Lured my serene, clairvoyant gaze to travel
To her belly and breasts, the grapes of my vine.

With a charm as powerful as an evil angel
To trouble the calm where my soul had retreated,
They advanced slowly to dislodge it from its crystal
Rock, where its loneliness meditated.

Je croyais voir unis par un nouveau dessin
Les hanches de l'Antiope au buste d'un imberbe,
Tant sa taille faisait ressortir son bassin.
Sur ce teint fauve et brun le fard était superbe !

— Et la lampe s'étant résignée à mourir,
Comme le foyer seul illuminait la chambre,
Chaque fois qu'il poussait un flamboyant soupir,
Il inondait de sang cette peau couleur d'ambre !

LE MASQUE

STATUE ALLÉGORIQUE DANS LE GOUT DE LA RENAISSANCE

A Ernest Christophe, statuaire.

Contemplons ce trésor de grâces florentines;
Dans l'ondulation de ce corps musculeux
L'Élégance et la Force abondent, sœurs divines.
Cette femme, morceau vraiment miraculeux,
Divinement robuste, adorablement mince,
Est faite pour trôner sur des lits somptueux,
Et charmer les loisirs d'un pontife ou d'un prince.

— Aussi, vois ce souris fin et voluptueux
Où la Fatuité promène son extase;
Ce long regard sournois, langoureux et moqueur;
Ce visage mignard, tout encadré de gaze,
Dont chaque trait nous dit avec un air vainqueur :
" La Volupté m'appelle et l'Amour me couronne ! "
A cet être doué de tant de majesté

With the hips of Antiope, the torso of a boy,
So deeply was the one form sprung into the other
It seemed as if desire had fashioned a new toy.
Her farded, fawn-brown skin was perfection to either !

— And the lamp having at last resigned itself to death,
There was nothing now but firelight in the room,
And every time a flame uttered a gasp for breath
It flushed her amber skin with the blood of its bloom.

— David Paul

THE MASK

AN ALLEGORICAL STATUE IN THE STYLE OF THE RENAISSANCE

To Ernest Christophe, sculptor.

Observe the Florentine grand style, and trace
How in this body's sinuous soft curves
Twin goddesses are present, Force and Grace;
Truly she is miraculous, deserves
In her delicious strength and suppleness
To be enthroned on some most sumptuous bed
And charm a king's or pontiff's idleness.

Observe again where self-conceit is led
To steal enjoyment from this tempting smile;
This languid, sinister and mocking air;
This coy regard, concealed beneath a veil,
In which victorious lineaments declare
" I am called Pleasure, and am crowned by Love. "
What thrilling charm informs her majesty

Vois quel charme excitant la gentillesse donne !
Approchons, et tournons autour de sa beauté.

O blasphème de l'art ! ô surprise fatale !
La femme au corps divin, promettant le bonheur,
Par le haut se termine en monstre bicéphale !

— Mais non ! ce n'est qu'un masque, un décor subor-
Ce visage éclairé d'une exquise grimace,   [neur,
Et, regarde, voici, crispée atrocement,
La véritable tête, et la sincère face
Renversée à l'abri de la face qui ment.
Pauvre grande beauté ! le magnifique fleuve
De tes pleurs aboutit dans mon cœur soucieux;
Ton mensonge m'enivre, et mon âme s'abreuve
Aux flots que la Douleur fait jaillir de tes yeux !

— Mais pourquoi pleure-t-elle ? Elle, beauté parfaite
Qui mettrait à ses pieds le genre humain vaincu,
Quel mal mystérieux ronge son flanc d'athlète ?

— Elle pleure, insensé, parce qu'elle a vécu !
Et parce qu'elle vit ! Mais ce qu'elle déplore
Surtout, ce qui la fait frémir jusqu'aux genoux,
C'est que demain, hélas ! il faudra vivre encore !
Demain, après-demain et toujours ! — comme nous !

This moving gentleness goes far to prove.
Let us go near and walk around her beauty.

Oh ! blasphemy of art ! Oh ! fatal shock !
The divine body, which appeared to ask
Us to our pleasure, has two heads that mock !

No ! these exquisite features are a mask,
Mere debased ornament with fine grimace;
Behind, atrociously contorted, is
The veritable head, the sincere face
Turned to the shadow of this face which lies.
Poor perfect beauty, a grand river breaks
As your tears fall into my anxious soul,
I am drunk with your lie, my spirit slakes
Its torture in the stream your eyes unroll.

Why is she weeping ? In her lovely pride
She could have conquered the whole race of man;
What unknown evil harrows her lithe side ?

She weeps, mad girl, because her life began;
Because she lives. One thing she does deplore
So much that she kneels trembling in the dust —
That she must live tomorrow, evermore,
Tomorrow and tomorrow — as we must !

— Graham Reynolds

HYMNE A LA BEAUTÉ

Viens-tu du ciel profond ou sors-tu de l'abîme,
O Beauté ? ton regard, infernal et divin,
Verse confusément le bienfait et le crime,
Et l'on peut pour cela te comparer au vin.

Tu contiens dans ton œil le couchant et l'aurore;
Tu répands des parfums comme un soir orageux;
Tes baisers sont un philtre et ta bouche une amphore
Qui font le héros lâche et l'enfant courageux.

Sors-tu du gouffre noir ou descends-tu des astres ?
Le Destin charmé suit tes jupons comme un chien;
Tu sèmes au hasard la joie et les désastres
Et tu gouvernes tout et ne réponds de rien.

Tu marches sur des morts, Beauté, dont tu te moques;
De tes bijoux l'Horreur n'est pas le moins charmant,
Et le Meurtre, parmi tes plus chères breloques,
Sur ton ventre orgueilleux danse amoureusement.

L'éphémère ébloui vole vers toi, chandelle,
Crépite, flambe et dit : Bénissons ce flambeau !
L'amoureux pantelant incliné sur sa belle
A l'air d'un moribond caressant son tombeau.

Que tu viennes du ciel ou de l'enfer, qu'importe,
O Beauté ! monstre énorme, effrayant, ingénu !
Si ton œil, ton souris, ton pied, m'ouvrent la porte
D'un Infini que j'aime et n'ai jamais connu ?

HYMN TO BEAUTY

From heaven or hell, O Beauty, come you hence ?
Out from your gaze, infernal and divine,
Pours blended evil and beneficence,
And therefore men have likened you to wine.

Sunset and dawn within your eyes are fair;
Stormlike you scatter perfume into space;
Your kiss, a philtre from an amphora rare,
Charms boys to courage and makes heroes base.

Whence come you, from what spheres, or inky deeps,
With careless hand joy and distress to strew ?
Fate, like a dog at heel, behind you creeps;
You govern all things here, and naught you rue.

You walk upon the dead with scornful glances,
Among your gems Horror is not least fair;
Murder, the dearest of your baubles, dances
Upon your haughty breast with amorous air.

Mothlike around your flame the transient, turning,
Crackles and flames and cries, " Ah, heavenly doom ! "
The quivering lover o'er his mistress yearning
Is but a dying man who woos his tomb.

From heaven or the abyss ? Let questioning be,
O artless monster wreaking endless pain,
So that your smile and glance throw wide to me
An infinite that I have loved in vain.

29

De Satan ou de Dieu, qu'importe ? Ange ou Sirène,
Qu'importe, si tu rends, — fée aux yeux de velours,
Rhythme, parfum, lueur, ô mon unique reine ! —
L'univers moins hideux et les instants moins lourds ?

LE SERPENT QUI DANSE

Que j'aime voir, chère indolente,
De ton corps si beau,
Comme une étoffe vacillante,
Miroiter la peau !

Sur ta chevelure profonde
Aux âcres parfums,
Mer odorante et vagabonde
Aux flots bleus et bruns,

Comme un navire qui s'éveille
Au vent du matin,
Mon âme rêveuse appareille
Pour un ciel lointain.

Tes yeux, où rien ne se révèle
De doux ni d'amer,
Sont deux bijoux froids où se mêle
L'or avec le fer.

From Satan or from God ? Holy or vile ?
Let questioning rest. O soft-eyed sprite, my queen,
O rhythm, perfume, light — so you beguile
Time from his slothfulness, the world from spleen.

— Dorothy Martin

THE DANCING SERPENT

Dear indolent, I love to see,
    In your body bright,
How like shimmering silk the skin
    Reflects the light !

On the deep ocean of your hair
    Where perfume laves,
Odorous and vagabond sea
    Of blue and brown waves,

Like a vessel awakening
    When morning winds rise
My dreaming soul begins to sail
    Toward remote skies.

Your two eyes that neither sweetness
    Nor bitterness hold
Are two chilly gems mingled of
    Iron and gold.

A te voir marcher en cadence,
   Belle d'abandon,
On dirait un serpent qui danse
   Au bout d'un bâton.

Sous le fardeau de ta paresse
   Ta tête d'enfant
Se balance avec la mollesse
   D'un jeune éléphant,

Et ton corps se penche et s'allonge
   Comme un fin vaisseau
Qui roule bord sur bord et plonge
   Ses vergues dans l'eau.

Comme un flot grossi par la fonte
   Des glaciers grondants,
Quand l'eau de ta bouche remonte
   Au bord de tes dents,

Je crois boire un vin de Bohême,
   Amer et vainqueur,
Un ciel liquide qui parsème
   D'étoiles mon cœur !

DE PROFUNDIS CLAMAVI

J'implore ta pitié, Toi, l'unique que j'aime,
Du fond du gouffre obscur où mon cœur est tombé.
C'est un univers morne à l'horizon plombé,
Où nagent dans la nuit l'horreur et le blasphème;

When you walk in rhythm, lovely
   With abandonment,
You seem to be swayed by a wand,
   A dancing serpent.

Your child's head under the burden
   Of your indolence
Sways as delicately as a
   Young elephant's,

And your body bends and straightens
   Like a slender ship
That, plunging and rolling, lets the
   Yards in water dip.

When, like a stream by thawing of
   Glaciers made replete,
The water of your mouth rises
   Up to your teeth,

I drink a Bohemian wine,
   Powerful and tart,
A liquid sky that sows its stars
   Within my heart !

                    — Barbara Gibbs

DE PROFUNDIS CLAMAVI

O my sole love, I pray thee pity me
From out this dark gulf where my poor heart lies,
A barren world hemmed in by leaden skies
Where horror flies at night, and blasphemy.

33

Un soleil sans chaleur plane au-dessus six mois,
Et les six autres mois la nuit couvre la terre;
C'est un pays plus nu que la terre polaire;
— Ni bêtes, ni ruisseaux, ni verdure, ni bois !

Or il n'est pas d'horreur au monde qui surpasse
La froide cruauté de ce soleil de glace
Et cette immense nuit semblable au vieux Chaos;

Je jalouse le sort des plus vils animaux
Qui peuvent se plonger dans un sommeil stupide,
Tant l'écheveau du temps lentement se dévide !

LE LÉTHÉ

Viens sur mon cœur, âme cruelle et sourde,
Tigre adoré, monstre aux airs indolents;
Je veux longtemps plonger mes doigts tremblants
Dans l'épaisseur de ta crinière lourde;

Dans tes jupons remplis de ton parfum
Ensevelir ma tête endolorie,
Et respirer, comme une fleur flétrie,
Le doux relent de mon amour défunt.

Je veux dormir ! dormir plutôt que vivre !
Dans un sommeil aussi doux que la mort,
J'étalerai mes baisers sans remord
Sur ton beau corps poli comme le cuivre.

34

For half the year the sickly sun is seen,
The other half thick night lies on the land,
A country bleaker than the polar strand;
No beasts, no brooks, nor any shred of green.

There never was a horror which surpassed
This icy sun's cold cruelty, and this vast
Night like primæval Chaos; would I were

Like the dumb brutes, who in a secret lair
Lie wrapt in stupid slumber for a space . . .
Time creeps at so burdensome a pace.

—Sir John Squire

LETHE

Come to my arms, cruel and sullen thing;
Indolent beast, come to my arms again,
For I would plunge my fingers in your mane
And be a long time unremembering —

And bury myself in you, and breathe your wild
Perfume remorselessly for one more hour :
And breathe again, as of a ruined flower,
The fragrance of the love you have defiled.

I long to sleep; I think that from a stark
Slumber like death I could awake the same
As I was once, and lavish without shame
Caresses upon your body, glowing and dark.

Pour engloutir mes sanglots apaisés
Rien ne vaut l'abîme de ta couche;
L'oubli puissant habite sur ta bouche,
Et le Léthé coule dans tes baisers.

A mon destin, désormais mon délice,
J'obéirai comme un prédestiné;
Martyr docile, innocent condamné,
Dont la ferveur attise le supplice,

Je sucerai, pour noyer ma rancoeur,
Le népenthès et la bonne ciguë
Aux bouts charmants de cette gorge aiguë,
Qui n'a jamais emprisonné de coeur.

REMORDS POSTHUME

Lorsque tu dormiras, ma belle ténébreuse,
Au fond d'un monument construit en marbre noir
Et lorsque tu n'auras pour alcôve et manoir
Qu'un caveau pluvieux et qu'une fosse creuse;

Quand la pierre, opprimant ta poitrine peureuse
Et tes flancs qu'assouplit un charmant nonchaloir,
Empêchera ton cœur de battre et de vouloir,
Et tes pieds de courir leur course aventureuse,

Le tombeau, confident de mon rêve infini
(Car le tombeau toujours comprendra le poëte),
Durant ces grandes nuits d'où le somme est banni,

To drown my sorrow there is no abyss,
However deep, that can compare with your bed.
Forgetfulness has made its country your red
Mouth, and the flowing of Lethe is in your kiss.

My doom, henceforward, is my sole desire :
As martyrs, being demented in their zeal,
Shake with delightful spasms upon the wheel,
Implore the whip, or puff upon the fire,

So I implore you, fervently resigned !
Come; I would drink nepenthe and long rest
At the sweet points of this entrancing breast
Wherein no heart has ever been confined.

— George Dillon

THE REMORSE OF THE DEAD

O shadowy Beauty mine, when thou shalt sleep
In the deep heart of a black marble tomb;
When thou for mansion and for bower shalt keep
Only one rainy cave of hollow gloom;

And when the stone upon thy trembling breast,
And on thy straight sweet body's supple grace,
Crushes thy will and keeps thy heart at rest,
And holds those feet from their adventurous race;

Then the deep grave, who shares my reverie,
(For the deep grave is ever the poet's friend)
During long nights when sleep is far from thee,

37

Te dira : " Que vous sert, courtisane imparfaite,
De n'avoir pas connu ce que pleurent les morts ? "
— Et le ver rongera ta peau comme un remords.

LE BALCON

Mère des souvenirs, maîtresse des maîtresses,
O toi, tous mes plaisirs ! ô toi, tous mes devoirs !
Tu te rappelleras la beauté des caresses,
La douceur du foyer et le charme des soirs,
Mère des souvenirs, maîtresse des maîtresses !

Les soirs illuminés par l'ardeur du charbon,
Et les soirs au balcon, voilés de vapeurs roses,
Que ton sein m'était doux ! que ton cœur m'était bon !
Nous avons dit souvent d'impérissables choses
Les soirs illuminés par l'ardeur du charbon.

Que les soleils sont beaux dans les chaudes soirées !
Que l'espace est profond ! Que le cœur est puissant !
En me penchant vers toi, reine des adorées,
Je croyais respirer le parfum de ton sang.
Que les soleils sont beaux dans les chaudes soirées !

La nuit s'épaississait ainsi qu'une cloison,
Et mes yeux dans le noir devinaient tes prunelles,
Et je buvais ton souffle, ô douceur ! ô poison !
Et tes pieds s'endormaient dans mes mains fraternelles.
La nuit s'épaississait ainsi qu'une cloison.

Shall whisper : " Ah, thou didst not comprehend
The dead wept thus, thou woman frail and weak " —
And like remorse the worm shall gnaw thy cheek.

—F. P. Sturm

THE BALCONY

Mother of memories, mistress of mistresses,
O thou, my pleasure, thou, all my desire,
Thou shalt recall the beauty of caresses,
The charm of evenings by the gentle fire,
Mother of memories, mistress of mistresses !

The eves illumined by the burning coal,
The balcony where veiled rose-vapour clings —
How soft your breast was then, how sweet your soul !
Ah, and we said imperishable things,
Those eves illumined by the burning coal.

Lovely the suns were in those twilights warm,
And space profound, and strong life's pulsing flood;
In bending o'er you, queen of every charm,
I thought I breathed the perfume of your blood.
The suns were beauteous in those twilights warm.

The film of night flowed round and over us,
And my eyes in the dark did your eyes meet;
I drank your breath, ah ! sweet and poisonous,
And in my hands fraternal slept your feet —
Night, like a film, flowed round and over us.

Je sais l'art d'évoquer les minutes heureuses,
Et revis mon passé blotti dans tes genoux.
Car à quoi bon chercher tes beautés langoureuses
Ailleurs qu'en ton cher corps et qu'en ton cœur si doux ?
Je sais l'art d'évoquer les minutes heureuses !

Ces serments, ces parfums, ces baisers infinis,
Renaîtront-ils d'un gouffre interdit à nos sondes,
Comme montent au ciel les soleils rajeunis
Après s'être lavés au fond des mers profondes ?
— O serments ! ô parfums ! ô baisers infinis !

RÉVERSIBILITÉ

Ange plein de gaieté, connaissez-vous l'angoisse,
La honte, les remords, les sanglots, les ennuis,
Et les vagues terreurs de ces affreuses nuits
Qui compriment le cœur comme un papier qu'on froisse ?
Ange plein de gaieté, connaissez-vous l'angoisse ?

Ange plein de bonté, connaissez-vous la haine,
Les poings crispés dans l'ombre et les larmes de fiel,
Quand la Vengeance bat son infernal rappel,
Et de nos facultés se fait le capitaine ?
Ange plein de bonté, connaissez-vous la haine ?

Ange plein de santé, connaissez-vous les Fièvres,
Qui, le long des grands murs de l'hospice blafard,

I can recall those happy days forgòt,
And see, with head bowed on your knees, my past.
Your languid beauties now would move me not
Did not your gentle heart and body cast
The old spell of those happy days forgot.

Can vows and perfume, kisses infinite,
Be reborn from the gulf we cannot sound;
As rise to heaven suns once again made bright
After being plunged in deep seas and profound ?
Ah, vows and perfumes, kisses infinite !

—F. P. Sturm

REVERSIBILITY

Angel of gaiety, have you tasted grief ?
Shame and remorse and sobs and weary spite,
And the vague terrors of the fearful night
That crush the heart up like a crumpled leaf ?
Angel of gaiety, have you tasted grief ?

Angel of kindness, have you tasted hate ?
With hands clenched in the dark, and tears of gall,
When Vengeance beats her hellish battle-call,
And makes herself the captain of our fate,
Angel of kindness, have you tasted hate ?

Angel of health, did ever you know pain,
Which like an exile trails his tired footfalls

Comme des exilés, s'en vont d'un pied traînard,
Cherchant le soleil rare et remuant les lèvres ?
Ange plein de santé, connaissez-vous les Fièvres ?

Ange plein de beauté, connaissez-vous les rides,
Et la peur de vieillir, et ce hideux tourment
De lire la secrète horreur du dévouement
Dans des yeux où longtemps burent nos yeux avides ?
Ange plein de beauté, connaissez-vous les rides ?

Ange plein de bonheur, de joie et de lumières,
David mourant aurait demandé la santé
Aux émanations de ton corps enchanté;
Mais de toi je n'implore, ange, que tes prières,
Ange plein de bonheur, de joie et de lumières !

CONFESSION

Une fois, une seule, aimable et douce femme,
    A mon bras votre bras poli
S'appuya (sur le fond ténébreux de mon âme
    Ce souvenir n'est point pâli);

Il était tard; ainsi qu'une médaille neuve
    La pleine lune s'étalait,
Et la solennité de la nuit, comme un fleuve,
    Sur Paris dormant ruisselait.

The cold length of the white infirmary walls,
With lips compressed, seeking the sun in vain ?
Angel of health, did ever you know pain ?

Angel of beauty, do you wrinkles know ?
Know you the fear of age, the torment vile
Of reading secret horror in the smile
Of eyes your eyes have loved since long ago ?
Angel of beauty, do you wrinkles know ?

Angel of happiness, and joy, and light,
Old David would have asked for youth afresh
From the pure touch of your enchanted flesh;
I but implore your prayers to aid my plight,
Angel of happiness, and joy, and light.

—F. P. Sturm

THE CONFESSION

Once, only once, beloved and gentle lady,
    Upon my arm you leaned your arm of snow,
And on my spirit's background, dim and shady,
    That memory flashes now.

The hour was late, and like a medal gleaming
    The full moon showed her face,
And the night's splendour over Paris streaming
    Filled every silent place.

43

Et le long des maisons, sous les portes cochères,
　　Des chats passaient furtivement,
L'oreille au guet, ou bien, comme des ombres chères,
　　Nous accompagnaient lentement.

Tout à coup, au milieu de l'intimité libre
　　Éclose à la pâle clarté,
De vous, riche et sonore instrument où ne vibre
　　Que la radieuse gaieté,

De vous, claire et joyeuse ainsi qu'une fanfare
　　Dans le matin étincelant,
Une note plaintive, une note bizarre
　　S'échappa tout en chancelant

Comme une enfant chétive, horrible, sombre, im-
　　Dont sa famille rougirait,　　　　　[monde,
Et qu'elle aurait longtemps, pour la cacher au monde,
　　Dans un caveau mise au secret.

Pauvre ange, elle chantait, votre note criarde :
　　" Que rien ici-bas n'est certain,
Et que toujours, avec quelque soin qu'il se farde,
　　Se trahit l'égoïsme humain ;

Que c'est un dur métier que d'être belle femme,
　　Et que c'est le travail banal
De la danseuse folle et froide qui se pâme
　　Dans un sourire machinal ;

44

Along the houses, in the doorways hiding,
    Cats passed with stealthy tread
And listening ear, or followed, slowly gliding,
    Like ghosts of dear ones dead.

Sudden, amid our frank and free relation,
    Born of that limpid light,
From you, rich instrument, whose sole vibration
    Was radiancy and light —

From you, joyous as bugle-call resounding
    Across the woods at morn,
With sharp and faltering accent, strangely sounding,
    Escaped one note forlorn.

Like some misshapen infant, dark, neglected,
    Its kindred blush to own,
And long have hidden, by no eye detected,
    In some dim cave unknown.

Your clashing note cried clear, poor, prisoned spirit,
    That nothing in the world is sure or fast,
And that man's selfishness, though decked as merit,
    Betrays itself at last.

That hard the lot to be a queen of beauty,
    And all is fruitless, like the treadmill toil
Of some paid dancer, fainting at her duty,
    Still with her vacant smile.

45

Que bâtir sur les cœurs est une chose sotte;
Que tout craque, amour et beauté,
Jusqu'à ce que l'Oubli les jette dans sa hotte
Pour les rendre à l'Éternité ! "

J'ai souvent évoqué cette lune enchantée,
Ce silence et cette langueur,
Et cette confidence horrible chuchotée
Au confessionnal du cœur.

LE FLACON

Il est de forts parfums pour qui toute matière
Est poreuse. On dirait qu'ils pénètrent le verre.
En ouvrant un coffret venu de l'Orient
Dont la serrure grince et rechigne en criant,

Ou dans une maison déserte quelque armoire
Pleine de l'âcre odeur des temps, poudreuse et noire,
Parfois on trouve un vieux flacon qui se souvient,
D'où jaillit toute vive une âme qui revient.

Mille pensers dormaient, chrysalides funèbres,
Frémissant doucement dans les lourdes ténèbres,
Qui dégagent leur aile et prennent leur essor,
Teintés d'azur, glacés de rose, lamés d'or.

46

That if one build on hearts, ill shall befall it,
   That all things crack, and love and beauty flee,
Until oblivion flings them in his wallet,
   Spoil of eternity.

Oft have I called to mind that night enchanted,
   The silence and the languor over all,
And that wild confidence, thus harshly chanted,
   At the heart's confessional.

                                    —Lois Saunders

THE FLASK

There are some powerful odours that can pass
Out of the stoppered flagon; even glass
To them is porous. Oft when some old box
Brought from the East is opened and the locks

And hinges creak and cry, or in a press
In some deserted house where the sharp stress
Of odours old and dusty fills the brain,
An ancient flask is brought to light again

And forth the ghosts of long-dead odours creep —
There, softly trembling in the shadows, sleep
A thousand thoughts, funereal chrysalides,
Phantoms of old the folding darkness hides,

47

Voilà le souvenir enivrant qui voltige
Dans l'air troublé; les yeux se ferment; le Vertige
Saisit l'âme vaincue et la pousse à deux mains
Vers un gouffre obscurci de miasmes humains;

Il la terrasse au bord d'un gouffre séculaire,
Où, Lazare odorant déchirant son suaire,
Se meut dans son réveil le cadavre spectral
D'un viel amour ranci, charmant et sépulcral.

Ainsi, quand je serai perdu dans la mémoire
Des hommes, dans le coin d'une sinistre armoire
Quand on m'aura jeté, vieux flacon désolé,
Décrépit, poudreux, sale, abject, visqueux, fêlé,

Je serai ton cercueil, aimable pestilence !
Le témoin de ta force et de ta virulence,
Cher poison préparé par les anges ! liqueur
Qui me ronge, ô la vie et la mort de mon cœur !

LE CHAT

I

Dans ma cervelle se promène,
Ainsi qu'en son appartement,
Un beau chat, fort, doux et charmant.
Quand il miaule, on l'entend à peine,

Who make faint flutterings as their wings unfold,
Rose-washed and azure-tinted, shot with gold.
A memory that brings languor flutters here :
The fainting eyelids droop, and giddy Fear

Thrusts with both hands the soul towards the pit
Where, like a Lazarus from his winding-sheet,
Arises from the gulf of sleep a ghost
Of an old passion, long since loved and lost.

So too, when vanished from man's memory
Deep in some dark and sombre chest I lie,
An empty flagon they have cast aside,
Broken and soiled, the dust upon my pride,

I'll be your shroud, beloved pestilence !
The witness of your might and virulence,
Sweet poison mixed by angels; bitter cup
Of life and death my heart has drunken up !

—F. P. Sturm

THE CAT

I

A fine strong gentle cat is prowling
As in his bedroom, in my brain;
So soft his voice, so smooth its strain,
That you can scarcely hear him miowling.

Tant son timbre est tendre et discret;
Mais que sa voix s'apaise ou gronde,
Elle est toujours riche et profonde.
C'est là son charme et son secret.

Cette voix qui perle et qui filtre
Dans mon fonds le plus ténébreux,
Me remplit comme un vers nombreux
Et me réjouit comme un philtre.

Elle endort les plus cruels maux
Et contient toutes les extases;
Pour dire les plus longues phrases,
Elle n'a pas besoin de mots.

Non, il n'est pas d'archet qui morde
Sur mon cœur, parfait instrument,
Et fasse plus royalement
Chanter sa plus vibrante corde,

Que ta voix, chat mystérieux,
Chat séraphique, chat étrange,
En qui tout est, comme en un ange,
Aussi subtil qu'harmonieux !

II

De sa fourrure blonde et brune
Sort un parfum si doux, qu'un soir
J'en fus embaumé, pour l'avoir
Caressée une fois, rien qu'une.

50

But should he venture to complain
Or scold, the voice is rich and deep :
And thus he manages to keep
The charm of his untroubled reign.

This voice, which seems to pearl and filter
Through my soul's inmost shady nook,
Fills me with poems, like a book,
And fortifies me, like a philtre.

His voice can cure the direst pain
And it contains the rarest raptures.
The deepest meanings, which it captures,
It needs no language to explain.

There is no bow that can so sweep
That perfect instrument, my heart :
Or make more sumptuous music start
From its most vibrant cord and deep,

Than can the voice of this strange elf,
This cat, bewitching and seraphic,
Subtly harmonious in his traffic
With all things else, and with himself.

II

So sweet a perfume seems to swim
Out of his fur both brown and bright,
I nearly was embalmed one night
From (only once) caressing him.

51

C'est l'esprit familier du lieu;
Il juge, il préside, il inspire
Toutes choses dans son empire;
Peut-être est-il fée, est-il dieu ?

Quand mes yeux, vers ce chat que j'aime
Tirés comme par un aimant,
Se retournent docilement
Et que je regarde en moi-même,

Je vois avec étonnement
Le feu de ses prunelles pâles,
Clairs fanaux, vivantes opales,
Qui me contemplent fixement.

L'INVITATION AU VOYAGE

Mon enfant, ma sœur,
Songe à la douceur
D'aller là-bas vivre ensemble !
Aimer à loisir,
Aimer et mourir
Au pays qui te ressemble !
Les soleils mouillés
De ces ciels brouillés
Pour mon esprit ont les charmes
Si mystérieux
De tes traîtres yeux,
Brillant à travers leurs larmes.

Familiar Lar of where I stay,
He rules, presides, inspires and teaches
All things to which his empire reaches.
Perhaps he is a god, or fay.

When to a cherished cat my gaze
Is magnet-drawn and then returns
Back to itself, it there discerns,
With strange excitement and amaze,

Deep down in my own self, the rays
Of living opals, torch-like gleams
And pallid fire of eyes, it seems,
That fixedly return my gaze.

— Roy Campbell

INVITATION TO THE VOYAGE

My child, my sister, dream
How sweet all things would seem
Were we in that kind land to live together,
And there love slow and long,
There love and die among
Those scenes that image you, that sumptuous weather.
Drowned suns that glimmer there
Through cloud-dishevelled air
Move me with such a mystery as appears
Within those other skies
Of your treacherous eyes
When I behold them shining through their tears.

53

Là, tout n'est qu'ordre et beauté,
Luxe, calme et volupté.

Des meubles luisants,
Polis par les ans,
Décoreraient notre chambre;
Les plus rares fleurs
Mêlant leurs odeurs
Aux vagues senteurs de l'ambre,
Les riches plafonds,
Les miroirs profonds,
La splendeur orientale,
Tout y parlerait
A l'âme en secret
Sa douce langue natale.

Là, tout n'est qu'ordre et beauté,
Luxe, calme et volupté.

Vois sur ces canaux
Dormir ces vaisseaux
Dont l'humeur est vagabonde;
C'est pour assouvir
Ton moindre désir
Qu'ils viennent du bout du monde.
— Les soleils couchants
Revêtent les champs,
Les canaux, la ville entière,
D'hyacinthe et d'or;
Le monde s'endort
Dans une chaude lumière.

Là, tout n'est qu'ordre et beauté,
Luxe, calme et volupté.

There, there is nothing else but grace and measure,
Richness, quietness, and pleasure.

Furniture that wears
The lustre of the years
Softly would glow within our glowing chamber,
Flowers of rarest bloom
Proffering their perfume
Mixed with the vague fragrances of amber;
Gold ceilings would there be,
Mirrors deep as the sea,
The walls all in an Eastern splendor hung —
Nothing but should address
The soul's loneliness,
Speaking her sweet and secret native tongue.

There, there is nothing else but grace and measure,
Richness, quietness, and pleasure.

See, sheltered from the swells
There in the still canals
Those drowsy ships that dream of sailing forth;
It is to satisfy
Your least desire, they ply
Hither through all the waters of the earth.
The sun at close of day
Clothes the fields of hay,
Then the canals, at last the town entire
In hyacinth and gold :
Slowly the land is rolled
Sleepward under a sea of gentle fire.

There, there is nothing else but grace and measure,
Richness, quietness, and pleasure.

— Richard Wilbur

CAUSERIE

Vous êtes un beau ciel d'automne, clair et rose !
Mais la tristesse en moi monte comme la mer,
Et laisse, en refluant, sur ma lèvre morose
Le souvenir cuisant de son !imon amer.

— Ta main se glisse en vain sur mon sein qui se pâme ;
Ce qu'elle cherche, amie, est un lieu saccagé
Par la griffe et la dent féroce de la femme.
Ne cherchez plus mon cœur ; les bêtes l'ont mangé.

Mon cœur est un palais flétri par la cohue ;
On s'y soûle, on s'y tue, on s'y prend aux cheveux !
— Un parfum nage autour de votre gorge nue !...

O Beauté, dur fléau des âmes, tu le veux !
Avec tes yeux de feu, brillants comme des fêtes,
Calcine ces lambeaux qu'ont épargnés les bêtes !

TRISTESSES DE LA LUNE

Ce soir, la lune rêve avec plus de paresse ;
Ainsi qu'une beauté, sur de nombreux coussins,
Qui d'une main discrète et légère caresse
Avant de s'endormir le contour de ses seins,

CONVERSATION

You are an autumn sky, suffused with rose . . .
Yet sadness rises in me like the sea,
And on my sombre lip, when it outflows,
Leaves its salt burning slime for memory.

Over my swooning breast your fingers stray;
In vain, alas ! My breast is a void pit
Sacked by the tooth and claw of woman. Nay,
Seek not my heart; the beasts have eaten it !

My heart is as a palace plundered
By the wolves, wherein they gorge and rend and kill,
A perfume round thy naked throat is shed . . .

Beauty, strong scourge of souls, O work thy will !
Scorch with thy fiery eyes which shine like feasts
These shreds of flesh rejected by the beasts !

— Sir John Squire

THE SADNESS OF THE MOON

The Moon more indolently dreams tonight
Than a fair woman on her couch at rest,
Caressing, with a hand distraught and light,
Before she sleeps, the contour of her breast.

Sur le dos satiné des molles avalanches,
Mourante, elle se livre aux longues pâmoisons,
Et promène ses yeux sur les visions blanches
Qui montent dans l'azur comme des floraisons.

Quand parfois sur ce globe, en sa langueur oisive,
Elle laisse filer une larme furtive,
Un poëte pieux, ennemi du sommeil,

Dans le creux de sa main prend cette larme pâle,
Aux reflets irisés comme un fragment d'opale,
Et la met dans son cœur loin des yeux du soleil.

LES HIBOUX

Sous les ifs noirs qui les abritent,
Les hiboux se tiennent rangés,
Ainsi que les dieux étrangers,
Dardant leur œil rouge. Ils méditent.

Sans remuer ils se tiendront
Jusqu'à l'heure mélancolique
Où, poussant le soleil oblique,
Les ténèbres s'établiront.

Leur attitude au sage enseigne
Qu'il faut en ce monde qu'il craigne
Le tumulte et le mouvement;

Upon her silken avalanche of down,
Dying she breathes a long and swooning sigh;
And watches the white visions past her flown,
Which rise like blossoms to the azure sky.

And when, at times, wrapped in her languor deep,
Earthward she lets a furtive tear-drop flow,
Some pious poet, enemy of sleep,

Takes in his hollow hand the tear of snow
Whence gleams of iris and of opal start,
And hides it from the Sun, deep in his heart.

—F. P. Sturm

THE OWLS

Within the shelter of black yews
The owls in ranks are ranged apart
Like foreign gods, whose eyeballs dart
Red fire. They meditate and muse.

Without a stir they will remain
Till, in its melancholy hour,
Thrusting the level sun from power,
The shade establishes its reign.

Their attitude instructs the sage,
Content with what is near at hand,
To shun all motion, strife, and rage.

59

L'homme ivre d'une ombre qui passe
Porte toujours le châtiment
D'avoir voulu changer de place.

LE MORT JOYEUX

Dans une terre grasse et pleine d'escargots
Je veux creuser moi-même une fosse profonde,
Où je puisse à loisir étaler mes vieux os
Et dormir dans l'oubli comme un requin dans l'onde.

Je hais les testaments et je hais les tombeaux;
Plutôt que d'implorer une larme du monde,
Vivant, j'aimerais mieux inviter les corbeaux
A saigner tous les bouts de ma carcasse immonde.

O vers ! noirs compagnons sans oreille et sans yeux,
Voyez venir à vous un mort libre et joyeux;
Philosophes viveurs, fils de la pourriture,

A travers ma ruine allez donc sans remords,
Et dites-moi s'il est encor quelque torture
Pour ce vieux corps sans âme et mort parmi les morts !

Men, crazed with shadows that they chase,
Bear, as a punishment, the brand
Of having wished to change their place.

— Roy Campbell

THE GLADLY DEAD

In a soil thick with snails and rich as grease
I've longed to dig myself a good deep grave,
There to stretch my old bones at ease
And sleep in oblivion, like a shark in a wave.

Wills I detest, and tombstones set in rows;
Before I'd beg a tear of anyone,
I'd rather go alive and let the crows
Bleed the last scrap of this old carrion.

O worms ! Black comrades without eye or ear,
Here comes a dead man for you, willing and gay;
Feasting philosophers, sons born of decay,

Come burrow through my ruins, shed not a tear;
But tell me if any torture is left to dread
For this old soulless body, dead as the dead ?

— Jackson Mathews

SPLEEN

Pluviôse, irrité contre la ville entière,
De son urne à grands flots verse un froid ténébreux
Aux pâles habitants du voisin cimetière
Et la mortalité sur les faubourgs brumeux.

Mon chat sur le carreau cherchant une litière
Agite sans repos son corps maigre et galeux;
L'âme d'un vieux poëte erre dans la gouttière
Avec la triste voix d'un fantôme frileux.

Le bourdon se lamente, et la bûche enfumée
Accompagne en fausset la pendule enrhumée,
Cependant qu'en un jeu plein de sales parfums,

Héritage fatal d'une vieille hydropique,
Le beau valet de cœur et la dame de pique
Causent sinistrement de leurs amours défunts.

SPLEEN

Quand le ciel bas et lourd pèse comme un couvercle
Sur l'esprit gémissant en proie aux longs ennuis,
Et que de l'horizon embrassant tout le cercle
Il nous verse un jour noir plus triste que les nuits;

SPLEEN

Old Pluvius, month of rains, in peevish mood
Pours from his urn chill winter's sodden gloom
On corpses fading in the near graveyard,
On foggy suburbs pours life's tedium.

My cat seeks out a litter on the stones,
Her mangy body turning without rest.
An ancient poet's soul in monotones
Whines in the rain-spouts like a chilblained ghost.

A great bell mourns, a wet log wrapped in smoke
Sings in falsetto to the wheezing clock,
While from a rankly perfumed deck of cards

(A dropsical old crone's fatal bequest)
The Queen of Spades, the dapper Jack of Hearts
Speak darkly of dead loves, how they were lost.

— Kenneth O. Hanson

SPLEEN

When the low heavy sky weighs like a lid
Upon the spirit aching for the light
And all the wide horizon's line is hid
By a black day sadder than any night;

Quand la terre est changée en un cachot humide,
Où l'Espérance, comme une chauve-souris,
S'en va battant les murs de son aile timide
Et se cognant la tête à des plafonds pourris;

Quand la pluie étalant ses immenses traînées
D'une vaste prison imite les barreaux,
Et qu'un peuple muet d'infâmes araignées
Vient tendre ses filets au fond de nos cerveaux,

Des cloches tout à coup sautent avec furie
Et lancent vers le ciel un affreux hurlement,
Ainsi que des esprits errants et sans patrie
Qui se mettent à geindre opiniâtrément.

— Et de longs corbillards, sans tambours ni musique,
Défilent lentement dans mon âme; l'Espoir,
Vaincu, pleure, et l'Angoisse atroce, despotique,
Sur mon crâne incliné plante son drapeau noir.

OBSESSION

Grands bois, vous m'effrayez comme des cathédrales;
Vous hurlez comme l'orgue; et dans nos cœurs maudits,
Chambres d'éternel deuil où vibrent de vieux râles,
Répondent les échos de vos *De profundis*.

When the changed earth is but a dungeon dank
Where batlike Hope goes blindly fluttering
And, striking wall and roof and mouldered plank,
Bruises his tender head and timid wing;

When like grim prison bars stretch down the thin,
Straight, rigid pillars of the endless rain,
And the dumb throngs of infamous spiders spin
Their meshes in the caverns of the brain,

Suddenly, bells leap forth into the air,
Hurling a hideous uproar to the sky
As 'twere a band of homeless spirits who fare
Through the strange heavens, wailing stubbornly.

And hearses, without drum or instrument,
File slowly through my soul; crushed, sorrowful,
Weeps Hope, and Grief, fierce and omnipotent,
Plants his black banner on my drooping skull.

— Sir John Squire

OBSESSION

You forests, like cathedrals, are my dread :
You roar like organs. Our curst hearts, like cells
Where death forever rattles on the bed,
Echo your *de Profundis* as it swells.

65

Je te hais, Océan ! tes bonds et tes tumultes,
Mon esprit les retrouve en lui; ce rire amer
De l'homme vaincu, plein de sanglots et d'insultes,
Je l'entends dans le rire énorme de la mer.

Comme tu me plairais, ô nuit ! sans ces étoiles
Dont la lumière parle un langage connu !
Car je cherche le vide, et le noir, et le nu !

Mais les ténèbres sont elles-mêmes des toiles
Où vivent, jaillissant de mon œil par milliers,
Des êtres disparus aux regards familiers.

L'HÉAUTONTIMOROUMÉNOS

A J. G. F.

Je te frapperai sans colère
Et sans haine, comme un boucher,
Comme Moïse le rocher !
Et je ferai de ta paupière,

Pour abreuver mon Saharah,
Jaillir les eaux de la souffrance.
Mon désir gonflé d'espérance
Sur tes pleurs salés nagera

Comme un vaisseau qui prend le large,
Et dans mon cœur qu'ils soûleront
Tes chers sanglots retentiront
Comme un tambour qui bat la charge

My spirit hates you, Ocean ! sees, and loathes
Its tumults in your own. Of men defeated
The bitter laugh, that's full of sobs and oaths,
Is in your own tremendously repeated.

How you would please me, Night ! without your stars
Which speak a foreign dialect, that jars
On one who seeks the void, the black, the bare.

Yet even your darkest shade a canvas forms
Whereon my eye must multiply in swarms
Familiar looks of shapes no longer there.

— Roy Campbell

HEAUTONTIMOROUMENOS

To J. G. F.

I'll strike you, but without the least
Anger — as butchers poll an ox,
Or Moses, when he struck the rocks —
That from your eyelid thus released,

The lymph of suffering may brim
To slake my desert of its drought.
So my desire, by hope made stout,
Upon your salty tears may swim,

Like a proud ship, far out from shore.
Within my heart, which they'll confound
With drunken joy, your sobs will sound
Like drums that beat a charge in war.

67

Ne suis-je pas un faux accord
Dans la divine symphonie,
Grâce à la vorace Ironie
Qui me secoue et qui me mord ?

Elle est dans ma voix, la criarde !
C'est tout mon sang, ce poison noir !
Je suis le sinistre miroir
Où la mégère se regarde!

Je suis la plaie et le couteau !
Je suis le soufflet et la joue !
Je suis les membres et la roue,
Et la victime et le bourreau !

Je suis de mon cœur le vampire,
— Un de ces grands abandonnés
Au rire éternel condamnés,
Et qui ne peuvent plus sourire !

L'IRRÉMÉDIABLE

I

Une Idée, une Forme, un Être
Parti de l'azur et tombé
Dans un Styx bourbeux et plombé
Où nul œil du Ciel ne pénètre;

Un Ange, imprudent voyageur
Qu'a tenté l'amour du difforme,

Am I not a faulty chord
In all this symphony divine,
Thanks to the irony malign
That shakes and cuts me like a sword ?

It's in my voice, the raucous jade !
It's in my blood's black venom too !
I am the looking-glass, wherethrough
Megaera sees herself portrayed !

I am the wound, and yet the blade !
The slap, and yet the cheek that takes it !
The limb, and yet the wheel that breaks it,
The torturer, and he who's flayed !

One of the sort whom all revile,
A Vampire, my own blood I quaff,
Condemned to an eternal laugh
Because I know not how to smile.

— Roy Campbell

THE IRREMEDIABLE

I

A Dream, a Form, a Creature, late
Fallen from azure realms, and sped
Into some Styx of mud and lead
No eye from heaven can penetrate;

An angel, rash wanderer, who craves
To look upon deformity,

Au fond d'un cauchemar énorme
Se débattant comme un nageur,

Et luttant, angoisses funèbres !
Contre un gigantesque remous
Qui va chantant comme les fous
Et pirouettant dans les ténèbres;

Un malheureux ensorcelé
Dans ses tâtonnements futiles,
Pour fuir d'un lieu plein de reptiles,
Cherchant la lumière et la clé;

Un damné descendant sans lampe,
Au bord d'un gouffre dont l'odeur
Trahit l'humide profondeur,
D'éternels escaliers sans rampe,

Où veillent des monstres visqueux
Dont les larges yeux de phosphore
Font une nuit plus noire encore
Et ne rendent visibles qu'eux;

Un navire pris dans le pôle,
Comme en un piége de cristal,
Cherchant par quel détroit fatal
Il est tombé dans cette geôle;

— Emblèmes nets, tableau parfait
D'une fortune irrémédiable,
Qui donne à penser que le Diable
Fait toujours bien tout ce qu'il fait !

The vast nightmare's gulf to try
As swimmer struggling with the waves,

And battling (anguish fierce and stark !)
Against gigantic whirlpools
That, singing, go like mad fools
Pirouetting in the dark;

One spellbound in sorcery,
Groping vainly as he makes
To flee a place alive with snakes,
Seeking the candle and the key;

A lost and lampless soul descending,
Within a gulf whose foetid scent
Betrays its damp and deep extent,
A railless staircase never ending,

Where clammy monsters guard the way,
Whose great eyes' phosphoric light
Makes even blacker still the night,
And nothing but themselves betray;

A vessel icebound at the pole,
As in a crystal trap secure,
Seeking the fatal aperture
By which it reached that prison goal :

— Perfect emblems, clear and true,
Of irremediable Fate,
They make us think the Devil's hate
Does well whatever he will do !

II

Tête-à-tête sombre et limpide
Qu'un cœur devenu son miroir !
Puits de Vérité, clair et noir,
Où tremble une étoile livide,

Un phare ironique, infernal,
Flambeau des grâces sataniques,
Soulagement et gloires uniques,
— La conscience dans le Mal !

L'HORLOGE

Horloge ! dieu sinistre, effrayant, impassible,
Dont le doigt nous menace et nous dit : *"Souviens-toi !*
Les vibrantes Douleurs dans ton cœur plein d'effroi
Se planteront bientôt comme dans une cible;

Le Plaisir vaporeux fuira vers l'horizon
Ainsi qu'une sylphide au fond de la coulisse;
Chaque instant te dévore un morceau du délice
A chaque homme accordé pour toute sa saison.

Trois mille six cents fois par heure, la Seconde
Chuchote : *Souviens-toi !* — Rapide, avec sa voix
D'insecte, Maintenant dit : Je suis Autrefois,
Et j'ai pompé ta vie avec ma trompe immonde !

II

The dialogue is dark and clear
When a heart becomes its mirror !
Black well of Truth, but none is clearer,
Where that livid star appears,

That ironic and primaeval
Beacon, torch of Satan's grace,
Our sole glory and our solace —
Consciousness in doing Evil !

— Henry Curwen

THE CLOCK

The Clock, calm evil god, that makes us shiver,
With threatening finger warns us each apart : —
" *Remember !* Soon the vibrant woes will quiver,
Like arrows in a target, in your heart.

To the horizon Pleasure will take flight
As flits a vaporous sylphide to the wings.
Each instant gnaws a crumb of the delight
That for his season every mortal brings.

Three thousand times and more, each hour, the second
Whispers ' *Remember !* ' Like an insect shrill
The present chirps, 'With Nevermore I'm reckoned.
I've pumped your lifeblood with my loathsome bill.'

73

Remember ! Souviens-toi ! prodigue ! *Esto memor !*
(Mon gosier de métal parle toutes les langues.)
Les minutes, mortel folâtre, sont des gangues
Qu'il ne faut pas lâcher sans en extraire l'or !

Souviens-toi que le Temps est un joueur avide
Qui gagne sans tricher, à tout coup ! c'est la loi.
Le jour décroît; la nuit augmente; *souviens-toi !*
Le gouffre a toujours soif; la clepsydre se vide.

Tantôt sonnera l'heure où le divin Hasard,
Où l'auguste Vertu, ton épouse encor vierge,
Où le Repentir même (oh ! la dernière auberge !),
Où tout te dira : Meurs, vieux lâche ! il est trop tard ! "

PAYSAGE

Je veux, pour composer chastement mes églogues,
Coucher auprès du ciel, comme les astrologues,
Et, voisin des clochers, écouter en rêvant
Leurs hymnes solennels emportés par le vent.
Les deux mains au menton, du haut de ma mansarde,
Je verrai l'atelier qui chante et qui bavarde;
Les tuyaux, les clochers, ces mâts de la cité,
Et les grands ciels qui font rêver d'éternité.

Il est doux, à travers les brumes, de voir naître
L'étoile dans l'azur, la lampe à la fenêtre,
Les fleuves de charbon monter au firmament
Et la lune verser son pâle enchantement.

Remember ! Souviens-toi ! Esto Memor !
My brazen windpipe speaks in every tongue.
Each moment, foolish mortal, is like ore
From which the precious metal must be wrung.

Remember. Time the gamester (it's the law)
Wins always, without cheating. Daylight wanes.
Night deepens. The abyss with gulfy maw
Thirsts on unsated, while the hourglass drains.

Sooner or later, now, the time must be
When Hazard, Virtue (your still-virgin mate),
Repentance (your last refuge), or all three —
Will tell you, 'Die, old Coward. It's too late ! ' "

— Roy Campbell

A LANDSCAPE

I would, when I compose my solemn verse,
Sleep near the heaven as do astrologers,
Near the high bells, and with a dreaming mind
Hear their calm hymns blown upon the wind.
Out of my tower, with chin upon my hands,
I'll watch the singing, babbling human bands;
And see clock-towers like spars against the sky,
And heavens that bring thoughts of eternity;

And softly, through the mist, will watch the birth
Of stars in heaven and lamplight on the earth;
The threads of smoke that rise above the town;
The moon that pours her pale enchantment down.

75

Je verrai les printemps, les étés, les automnes,
Et quand viendra l'hiver aux neiges monotones,
Je fermerai partout portières et volets
Pour bâtir dans la nuit mes féeriques palais.
Alors je rêverai des horizons bleuâtres,
Des jardins, des jets d'eau pleurant dans les albâtres,
Des baisers, des oiseaux chantant soir et matin,
Et tout ce que l'Idylle a de plus enfantin.
L'Émeute, tempêtant vainement à ma vitre,
Ne fera pas lever mon front de mon pupitre;
Car je serai plongé dans cette volupté
D'évoquer le Printemps avec ma volonté,
De tirer un soleil de mon cœur, et de faire
De mes pensers brûlants une tiède atmosphère.

LE SOLEIL

Le long du vieux faubourg, où pendent aux masures
Les persiennes, abri des secrètes luxures,
Quand le soleil cruel frappe à traits redoublés
Sur la ville et les champs, sur les toits et les blés,
Je vais m'exercer seul à ma fantasque escrime,
Flairant dans tous les coins les hasards de la rime,
Trébuchant sur les mots comme sur les pavés,
Heurtant parfois des vers depuis longtemps rêvés.

Ce père nourricier, ennemi des chloroses,
Éveille dans les champs les vers comme les roses;

Seasons will pass till Autumn fades the rose;
And when comes Winter with his weary snows,
I'll shut the doors and window-casements tight,
And build my faery palace in the night.
Then I will dream of blue horizons deep,
Of gardens where the marble fountains weep,
Of kisses, and of ever-singing birds —
A sinless Idyll built of innocent words.
And Trouble, knocking at my window-pane
And at my closet door, shall knock in vain;
I will not heed him with his stealthy tread,
Nor from my reverie uplift my head;
For I will plunge deep in the pleasure still
Of summoning the spring-time with my will,
Drawing the sun out of my heart, and there
With burning thoughts making a summer air.

—F. P. Sturm

THE SUN

Along old terraces where blinds tent the masonry
Each one a separate shelter for private luxury,
When the cruel sun redoubles its sharp stroke
On street and hedgerow, on rooftop and brake,
I walk alone, absorbed in my curious exercise,
Duelling with words that dodge in corners and byways;
Stumbling on rhymes as on crooked setts, colliding
With a sudden clear line which dreams were past finding.

The all-satisfying sun, anaemia's enemy,
Gives life to the worm and the rose impartially;

77

Il fait s'évaporer les soucis vers le ciel,
Et remplit les cerveaux et les ruches de miel.
C'est lui qui rajeunit les porteurs de béquilles
Et les rend gais et doux comme des jeunes filles,
Et commande aux moissons de croître et de mûrir
Dans le cœur immortel qui toujours veut fleurir !

Quand, ainsi qu'un poëte, il descend dans les villes,
Il ennoblit le sort des choses les plus viles,
Et s'introduit en roi, sans bruit et sans valets,
Dans tous les hôpitaux et dans tous les palais.

LE CYGNE

A Victor Hugo.

I

Andromaque, je pense à vous ! Ce petit fleuve,
Pauvre et triste miroir où jadis resplendit
L'immense majesté de vos douleurs de veuve,
Ce Simoïs menteur qui par vos pleurs grandit,

A fécondé soudain ma mémoire fertile,
Comme je traversais le nouveau Carrousel.
Le vieux Paris n'est plus (la forme d'une ville
Change plus vite, hélas ! que le cœur d'un mortel);

Je ne vois qu'en esprit tout ce camp de baraques,
Ces tas de chapiteaux ébauchés et de fûts,

Evaporating care and sending it skywards
He brings honey to the hive, and to the mute mind words.
It is he who makes the ancient cripples young again
With the gaiety and gentleness of young children;
He orders the harvest to increase and flourish
In that old heart where life is the perpetual wish.

When he comes down into the city like a poet
Transfiguring the values of things the most abject,
He enters like royalty, unaccompanied by officials,
All the palatial hotels and all the hospitals.

— David Paul

THE SWAN

To Victor Hugo.

I

Andromache, I think of you ! The stream,
The poor, sad mirror where in bygone days
Shone all the majesty of your widowed grief,
The lying Simoïs flooded by your tears,

Made all my fertile memory blossom forth
As I passed by the new-built Carrousel.
Old Paris is no more (a town, alas,
Changes more quickly than man's heart may change);

Yet in my mind I still can see the booths;
The heaps of brick and rough-hewn capitals;

79

Les herbes, les gros blocs verdis par l'eau des flaques,
Et, brillant aux carreaux, le bric-à-brac confus.

Là s'étalait jadis une ménagerie;
Là je vis, un matin, à l'heure où sous les cieux
Froids et clairs le Travail s'éveille, où la voirie
Pousse un sombre ouragan dans l'air silencieux,

Un cygne qui s'était évadé de sa cage,
Et, de ses pieds palmés frottant le pavé sec,
Sur le sol raboteux traînait son blanc plumage.
Près d'un ruisseau sans eau la bête ouvrant le bec

Baignait nerveusement ses ailes dans la poudre,
Et disait, le cœur plein de son beau lac natal :
" Eau, quand donc pleuvras-tu ? quand tonneras-tu,
Je vois ce malheureux, mythe étrange et fatal, [foudre?''

Vers le ciel quelquefois, comme l'homme d'Ovide,
Vers le ciel ironique et crullement bleu,
Sur son cou convulsif tendant sa tête avide,
Comme s'il adressait des reproches à Dieu !

II

Paris change ! mais rien dans ma mélancolie
N'a bougé ! palais neufs, échafaudages, blocs,
Vieux faubourgs, tout pour moi devient allégorie,
Et mes chers souvenirs sont plus lourds que des rocs.

Aussi devant ce Louvre une image m'opprime :
Je pense à mon grand cygne, avec ses gestes fous,

The grass; the stones all over-green with moss;
The débris, and the square-set heaps of tiles.

There a menagerie was once outspread;
And there I saw, one morning at the hour
When Toil awakes beneath the cold, clear sky,
And the road roars upon the silent air,

A swan who had escaped his cage, and walked
On the dry pavement with his webby feet,
And trailed his spotless plumage on the ground.
And near a waterless stream the piteous swan
Opened his beak, and bathing in the dust
His nervous wings, he cried (his heart the while
Filled with a vision of his own fair lake) :
" O water, when then wilt thou come in rain ?
Lightning, when wilt thou glitter ? "
                                        Sometimes yet
I see the hapless bird — strange, fatal myth —
Like him that Ovid writes of, lifting up
Unto the cruelly blue, ironic heavens,
With stretched, convulsive neck a thirsty face,
As though he sent reproaches up to God !

II

Paris may change; my melancholy is fixed.
New palaces, and scaffoldings, and blocks,
And suburbs old, are symbols all to me
Whose memories are as heavy as a stone.
And so, before the Louvre, to vex my soul,
The image came of my majestic swan

81

Comme les exilés, ridicule et sublime,
Et rongé d'un désir sans trêve ! et puis à vous,

Andromaque, des bras d'un grand époux tombée,
Vil bétail, sous la main du superbe Pyrrhus,
Auprès d'un tombeau vide en extase courbée ;
Veuve d'Hector, hélas ! et femme d'Hélénus !

Je pense à la négresse, amaigrie et phthisique,
Piétinant dans la boue, et cherchant, l'œil hagard,
Les cocotiers absents de la superbe Afrique
Derrière la muraille immense du brouillard ;

A quiconque a perdu ce qui ne se retrouve
Jamais, jamais ! à ceux qui s'abreuvent de pleurs
Et tettent la Douleur comme une bonne louve !
Aux maigres orphelins séchant comme des fleurs !

Ainsi dans la forêt où mon esprit s'exile
Un vieux Souvenir sonne à plein souffle du cor !
Je pense aux matelots oubliés dans une île,
Aux captifs, aux vaincus !... à bien d'autres encor !

LES SEPT VIEILLARDS

A Victor Hugo.

Fourmillante cité, cité pleine de rêves,
Où le spectre, en plein jour, raccroche le passant !
Les mystères partout coulent comme des séves
Dans les canaux étroits du colosse puissant.

With his mad gestures, foolish and sublime,
As of an exile whom one great desire
Gnaws with no truce. And then I thought of you,
Andromache ! torn from your hero's arms;
Beneath the hand of Pyrrhus in his pride;
Bent o'er an empty tomb in ecstasy;
Widow of Hector — wife of Helenus !
And of the Negress, wan and phthisical,
Tramping the mud, and with her haggard eyes
Seeking beyond the mighty walls of fog
The absent palm-trees of proud Africa;
Of all who lose that which they never find;
Of all who drink of tears; all whom grey Grief
Gives suck to as the kindly wolf gave suck;
Of meagre orphans who like blossoms fade.

And one old Memory like a crying horn
Sounds through the forest where my soul is lost . . .
I think of sailors on some isle, forgotten;
Of captives, vanquished . . . and of many more.

—F. P. Sturm

THE SEVEN OLD MEN

To Victor Hugo.

Ant-seething city, city full of dreams,
Where ghosts by daylight tug the passer's sleeve.
Mystery, like sap, through all its conduit-streams,
Quickens the dread Colossus that they weave.

83

Un matin, cependant que dans la triste rue
Les maisons, dont la brume allongeait la hauteur,
Simulaient les deux quais d'une rivière accrue,
Et que, décor semblable à l'âme de l'acteur,

Un brouillard sale et jaune inondait tout l'espace,
Je suivais, roidissant mes nerfs comme un héros
Et discutant avec mon âme déjà lasse,
Le faubourg secoué par les lourds tombereaux.

Tout à coup, un vieillard dont les guenilles jaunes
Imitaient la couleur de ce ciel pluvieux,
Et dont l'aspect aurait fait pleuvoir les aumônes,
Sans la méchanceté qui luisait dans ses yeux,

M'apparut. On eût dit sa prunelle trempée
Dans le fiel; son regard aiguisait les frimas,
Et sa barbe à longs poils, roide comme une épée,
Se projetait, pareille à celle de Judas.

Il n'était pas voûté, mais cassé, son échine
Faisant avec sa jambe un parfait angle droit,
Si bien que son bâton, parachevant sa mine,
Lui donnait la tournure et le pas maladroit

D'un quadrupède infirme ou d'un juif à trois pattes.
Dans la neige et la boue il allait s'empêtrant,
Comme s'il écrasait des morts sous ses savates,
Hostile à l'univers plutôt qu'indifférent.

Son pareil le suivait : barbe, œil, dos, bâton, loques,
Nul trait ne distinguait, du même enfer venu,

One early morning, in the street's sad mud,
Whose houses, by the fog increased in height,
Seemed wharves along a riverside in flood :
When with a scene to match the actor's plight,

Foul yellow mist had filled the whole of space :
Steeling my nerves to play a hero's part,
I coaxed my weary soul with me to pace
The backstreets shaken by each lumbering cart.

A wretch appeared whose tattered, yellow clothing,
Matching the colour of the raining sky,
Could make it shower down alms — but for the loathing
Malevolence that glittered in his eye.

The pupils of his eyes, with bile injected,
Seemed with their glance to make the frost more raw.
Stiff as a sword, his long red beard projected,
Like that of Judas, level with his jaw.

He was not bent, but broken, with the spine
Forming a sharp right-angle to the straight,
So that his stick, to finish the design,
Gave him the stature and the crazy gait

Of a three-footed Jew, or crippled hound.
He plunged his soles into the slush as though
To crush the dead; and to the world around
Seemed less of an indifferent than a foe.

His image followed him (back, stick, and beard
In nothing differed), spawned from the same hole,

Ce jumeau centenaire, et ces spectres baroques
Marchaient du même pas vers un but inconnu.

A quel complot infâme étais-je donc en butte,
Ou quel méchant hasard ainsi m'humiliait ?
Car je comptai sept fois, de minute en minute,
Ce sinistre vieillard qui se multipliait !

Que celui-là qui rit de mon inquiétude,
Et qui n'est pas saisi d'un frisson fraternel,
Songe bien que malgré tant de décrépitude
Ces sept monstres hideux avaient l'air éternel !

Aurais-je, sans mourir, contemplé le huitième,
Sosie inexorable, ironique et fatal,
Dégoûtant Phénix, fils et père de lui-même ?
— Mais je tournai le dos au cortége infernal.

Exaspéré comme un ivrogne qui voit double,
Je rentrai, je fermai ma porte, épouvanté,
Malade et morfondu, l'esprit fiévreux et trouble,
Blessé par le mystère et par l'absurdité !

Vainement ma raison voulait prendre la barre;
La tempête en jouant déroutait ses efforts,
Et mon âme dansait, dansait, vieille gabarre
Sans mâts, sur une mer monstrueuse et sans bords !

A centenarian twin. Both spectres steered
With the same gait to the same unknown goal.

To what foul plot was I exposed ? of what
Humiliating hazard made the jeer ?
For seven times (I counted) was begot
This sinister, self-multiplying fear !

Let him mark well who laughs at my despair
With no fraternal shudder in reply . . .
Those seven loathsome monsters had the air,
Though rotting through, of what can never die

Disgusting Phoenix, his own son and father !
Could I have watched an eighth instalment spawn
Ironic, fateful, grim — nor perished rather ?
But from that hellish cortege I'd withdrawn.

Perplexed as drunkards when their sight is doubled,
I locked my room, sick, fevered, chilled with fright :
With all my spirit sorely hurt and troubled
By so ridiculous yet strange a sight.

Vainly my reason for the helm was striving :
The tempest of my efforts made a scorn.
My soul like a dismasted wreck went driving
Over a monstrous sea without a bourn.

— Roy Campbell

LES PETITES VIEILLES

A Victor Hugo.

I

Dans les plis sinueux des vieilles capitales,
Où tout, même l'horreur, tourne aux enchantements,
Je guette, obéissant à mes humeurs fatales,
Des êtres singuliers, décrépits et charmants.

Ces monstres disloqués furent jadis des femmes,
Éponine ou Laïs ! Monstres brisés, bossus
Ou tordus, aimons-les ! ce sont encor des âmes.
Sous des jupons troués ou sous de froids tissus

Ils rampent, flagellés par les bises iniques,
Frémissant au fracas roulant des omnibus,
Et serrant sur leur flanc, ainsi que des reliques,
Un petit sac brodé de fleurs ou de rébus ;

Ils trottent, tous pareils à des marionnettes ;
Se traînent, comme font les animaux blessés,
Ou dansent, sans vouloir danser, pauvres sonnettes
Où se pend un Démon sans pitié ! Tout cassés

Qu'ils sont, ils ont des yeux perçants comme une vrille,
Luisants comme ces trous où l'eau dort dans la nuit ;
Ils ont les yeux divins de la petite fille
Qui s'étonne et qui rit à tout ce qui reluit.

— Avez-vous observé que maints cercueils de vieilles
Sont presque aussi petits que celui d'un enfant ?
La Mort savante met dans ces bières pareilles
Un symbole d'un goût bizarre et captivant,

THE LITTLE OLD WOMEN

To Victor Hugo.

I

In sinuous folds of cities old and grim,
Where all things, even horror, turn to grace,
I follow, in obedience to my whim,
Strange, feeble, charming creatures round the place.

These crooked freaks were women in their pride,
Fair Eponine or Laïs ! Humped and bent,
Love them ! Because they still have souls inside.
Under their draughty skirts in tatters rent,

They crawl : a vicious wind their carrion rides;
From the deep roar of traffic see them cower,
Pressing like precious relics to their sides
Some satchel stitched with mottoes or a flower.

They trot like marionettes along the level,
Or drag themselves like wounded deer, poor crones !
Or dance, against their will, as if the devil
Were swinging in the belfry of their bones.

Cracked though they are, their eyes are sharp as drills
And shine, like pools of water in the night, —
The eyes of little girls whom wonder thrills
To laugh at all that sparkles and is bright.

The coffins of old women very often
Are near as small as those of children are.
Wise Death, who makes a symbol of a coffin
Displays a taste both charming and bizarre.

Et lorsque j'entrevois un fantôme débile
Traversant de Paris le fourmillant tableau,
Il me semble toujours que cet être fragile
S'en va tout doucement vers un nouveau berceau;

A moins que, méditant sur la géométrie,
Je ne cherche, à l'aspect de ces membres discords,
Combien de fois il faut que l'ouvrier varie
La forme de la boîte où l'on met tous ces corps.

— Ces yeux sont des puits faits d'un million de larmes,
Des creusets qu'un métal refroidi pailleta...
Ces yeux mystérieux ont d'invincibles charmes
Pour celui que l'austère infortune allaita !

II

De Frascati défunt Vestale enamourée;
Prêtresse de Thalie, hélas ! dont le souffleur
Enterré sait le nom; célèbre évaporée
Que Tivoli jadis ombragea dans sa fleur,

Toutes m'enivrent ! mais parmi ces êtres frêles
Il en est qui, faisant de la douleur un miel,
Ont dit au Dévouement qui leur prêtait ses ailes :
Hippogriffe puissant, mène-moi jusqu'au ciel !

L'une, par sa patrie au malheur exercée,
L'autre, que son époux surchargea de douleurs,
L'autre, par son enfant Madone transpercée,
Toutes auraient pu faire un fleuve avec leurs pleurs !

And when I track some feeble phantom fleeing
Through Paris's immense ant-swarming Babel,
I always think that such a fragile being
Is moving softly to another cradle.

Unless, sometimes, in geometric mood,
To see the strange deformities they offer,
I muse how often he who saws the wood
Must change the shape and outline of the coffer.

Those eyes are wells a million teardrops feed,
Crucibles spangled by a cooling ore,
Invincible in charm to all that breed
Whom stern Misfortune suckled with her lore.

II

Vestal whom old Frascati could enamour :
Thalia's nun, whose name was only known
To her dead prompter : madcap full of glamour
Whom Tivoli once sheltered as its own —

They all elate me. But of these a few,
Of sorrow having made a honeyed leaven,
Say to Devotion, " Lend me wings anew,
O powerful Hippogriff, and fly to heaven."

One for her fatherland a martyr : one
By her own husband wronged beyond belief :
And one a pierced Madonna through her son —
They all could make a river with their grief.

91

III

Ah ! que j'en ai suivi de ces petites vieilles !
Une, entre autres, à l'heure où le soleil tombant
Ensanglante le ciel de blessures vermeilles,
Pensive, s'asseyait à l'écart sur un banc,

Pour entendre un de ces concerts, riches de cuivre,
Dont les soldats parfois inondent nos jardins,
Et qui, dans ces soirs d'or où l'on se sent revivre,
Versent quelque héroïsme au cœur des citadins.

Celle-là, droite encor, fière et sentant la règle,
Humait avidement ce chant vif et guerrier;
Son œil parfois s'ouvrait comme l'œil d'un vieil aigle;
Son front de marbre avait l'air fait pour le laurier !

IV

Telles vous cheminez, stoïques et sans plaintes,
A travers le chaos des vivantes cités,
Mères au cœur saignant, courtisanes ou saintes,
Dont autrefois les noms par tous étaient cités.

Vous qui fûtes la grâce ou qui fûtes la gloire,
Nul ne vous reconnaît ! un ivrogne incivil
Vous insulte en passant d'un amour dérisoire;
Sur vos talons gambade un enfant lâche et vil.

Honteuses d'exister, ombres ratatinées,
Peureuses, le dos bas, vous côtoyez les murs;
Et nul ne vous salue, étranges destinées !
Débris d'humanité pour l'éternité mûrs !

III

Yes, I have followed them, time and again !
One, I recall, when sunset, like a heart,
Bled through the sky from wounds of ruddy stain,
Pensively sat upon a seat apart,

To listen to the music, rich in metal,
That's played by bands of soldiers in the parks
On golden, soul-reviving eves, to fettle,
From meek civilian hearts, heroic sparks.

This one was straight and stiff, in carriage regal,
She breathed the warrior-music through her teeth,
Opened her eye like that of an old eagle,
And bared a forehead moulded for a wreath.

IV

Thus then, you journey, uncomplaining, stoic
Across the strife of modern cities flung,
Sad mothers, courtesans, or saints heroic,
Whose names of old were heard on every tongue,

You once were grace, and you were glory once.
None know you now. Derisory advances
Some drunkard makes you, mixed with worse affronts.
And on your heels a child-tormentor prances.

Ashamed of living, shrivelled shades, who creep
Timidly sidling by the walls, bent double;
Nobody greets you, ripe for endless sleep,
Strange destinies, and shards of human rubble !

Mais moi, moi qui de loin tendrement vous surveille,
L'œil inquiet fixé sur vos pas incertains,
Tout comme si j'étais votre père, ô merveille !
Je goûte à votre insu des plaisirs clandestins :

Je vois s'épanouir vos passions novices;
Sombres ou lumineux, je vis vos jours perdus;
Mon cœur multiplié jouit de tous vos vices !
Mon âme resplendit de toutes vos vertus !

Ruines ! ma famille ! ô cerveaux congénères !
Je vous fais chaque soir un solennel adieu !
Où serez-vous demain, Èves octogénaires,
Sur qui pèse la griffe effroyable de Dieu ?

LE SQUELETTE LABOUREUR

De ce terrain que vous fouillez,
Manants résignés et funèbres,
De tout l'effort de vos vertèbres,
Ou de vos muscles dépouillés,

Dites, quelle moisson étrange,
Forçats arrachés au charnier,
Tirez-vous, et de quel fermier
Avez-vous à remplir la grange ?

94

But I who watch you tenderly : and measure
With anxious eye, your weak unsteady gait
As would a father — get a secret pleasure
On your account, as on your steps I wait.

I see your passionate and virgin crazes;
Sombre or bright, I see your vanished prime;
My soul, resplendent with your virtue, blazes,
And revels in your vices and your crimes.

Poor wrecks ! My family ! Kindred in mind, you
Receive from me each day my last addresses.
Eighty-year Eves, will yet tomorrow find you
On whom the claw of God so fiercely presses ?

— Roy Campbell

THE SKELETON LABORER

*Written to the flayed and fleshless figures on an
anatomical chart, from the 19th century French.*

Out of the earth at which you spade,
Funereal laborers, tired and done,
Out of your straining naked bone,
Out of your muscles bare and frayed,

Tell me, what harvest do you win?
Slaves snatched from the charnel ground,
Who is the farmer drives this round
To fill his barn? And what your sin?

95

Voulez-vous (d'un destin trop dur
Épouvantable et clair emblème !)
Montrer que dans la fosse même
Le sommeil promis n'est pas sûr;

Qu'envers nous le Néant est traître;
Que tout, même la Mort, nous ment,
Et que sempiternellement,
Hélas ! il nous faudra peut-être

Dans quelque pays inconnu
Écorcher la terre revêche
Et pousser une lourde bêche
Sous notre pied sanglant et nu ?

LE CRÉPUSCULE DU SOIR

Voici le soir charmant, ami du criminel;
Il vient comme un complice, à pas de loup; le ciel
Se ferme lentement comme une grande alcôve,
Et l'homme impatient se change en bête fauve.

O soir, aimable soir, désiré par celui
Dont les bras, sans mentir, peuvent dire : Aujourd'hui
Nous avons travaillé ! — C'est le soir qui soulage
Les esprits que dévore une douleur sauvage,
Le savant obstiné dont le front s'alourdit,
Et l'ouvrier courbé qui regagne son lit.
Cependant des démons malsains dans l'atmosphère

You, the terrible sign we're shown
Of our destiny's greater dearth,
Wish you to say that in the earth
The promised sleep is never known?

That the end has betrayed us here,
That even death himself has lied?
That though eternity betide,
Alas! we have again to fear

That in some unknown land we'll meet
A knotted earth that needs to be flayed —
To drive again the heavy spade
Beneath our bleeding naked feet?

— Yvor Winters

COMES THE CHARMING EVENING

Comes the charming evening, the criminal's friend,
Comes conspirator-like on soft wolf tread.
Like a large alcove the sky slowly closes,
And man approaches his bestial metamorphosis.

To arms that have laboured, evening is kind enough,
Easing the strain of sinews that have borne their rough
Share of the burden; it is evening that relents
To those whom an angry obsession daily haunts.
The solitary student now raises a burdened head
And the back that bent daylong sinks into its bed.
Meanwhile darkness dawns, filled with demon familiars

97

S'éveillent lourdement, comme des gens d'affaire,
Et cognent en volant les volets et l'auvent.

A travers les lueurs que tourmente le vent
La Prostitution s'allume dans les rues;
Comme une fourmilière elle ouvre ses issues;
Partout elle se fraye un occulte chemin,
Ainsi que l'ennemi qui tente un coup de main;
Elle remue au sein de la cité de fange
Comme un ver qui dérobe à l'Homme ce qu'il mange.
On entend çà et là les cuisines siffler,
Les théâtres glapir, les orchestres ronfler;
Les tables d'hôte, dont le jeu fait les délices,
S'emplissent de catins et d'escrocs, leurs complices,
Et les voleurs, qui n'ont ni trêve ni merci,
Vont bientôt commencer leur travail, eux aussi,
Et forcer doucement les portes et les caisses
Pour vivre quelques jours et vêtir leurs maîtresses.

Recueille-toi, mon âme, en ce grave moment,
Et ferme ton oreille à ce rugissement.
C'est l'heure où les douleurs des malades s'aigrissent!
La sombre Nuit les prend à la gorge; ils finissent
Leur destinée et vont vers le gouffre commun;
L'hôpital se remplit de leurs soupirs. — Plus d'un
Ne viendra plus chercher la soupe parfumée,
Au coin du feu, le soir, auprès d'une âme aimée.

Encore la plupart n'ont-ils jamais connu
La douceur du foyer et n'ont jamais vécu!

Who rouse, reluctant as business-men, to their affairs,
Their ponderous flight rattling the shutters and blinds.
Against the lamplight, whose shivering is the wind's,
Prostitution spreads its light and life in the streets :
Like an anthill opening its issues it penetrates
Mysteriously everywhere by its own occult route;
Like an enemy mining the foundations of a fort,
Or a worm in an apple, eating what all should eat,
It circulates securely in the city's clogged heart.
The heat and hiss of kitchens can be felt here and there,
The panting of heavy bands, the theatres' clamour.
Cheap hotels, the haunts of dubious solaces,
Are filling with tarts, and crooks, their sleek accomplices,
And thieves, who have never heard of restraint or remorse,
Return now to their work as a matter of course,
Forcing safes behind carefully re-locked doors,
To get a few days' living and put clothes on their whores.

Collect yourself, my soul, this is a serious moment,
Pay no further attention to the noise and movement.
This is the hour when the pains of the sick sharpen,
Night touches them like a torturer, pushes them to the open
Trapdoor over the gulf that is all too common.
Their groans overflow the hospital. More than one
Will not come back to taste the soup's familiar flavour
In the evening, with some friendly soul, by his own fire.

Indeed, many a one has never even known
The hearth's warm charm. Pity such a one.

— David Paul

LE JEU

Dans des fauteuils fanés des courtisanes vieilles,
Pâles, le sourcil peint, l'œil câlin et fatal,
Minaudant, et faisant de leurs maigres oreilles
Tomber un cliquetis de pierre et de métal;

Autour des verts tapis des visages sans lèvre,
Des lèvres sans couleur, des mâchoires sans dent,
Et des doigts convulsés d'une infernale fièvre,
Fouillant la poche vide ou le sein palpitant;

Sous de sales plafonds un rang de pâles lustres
Et d'énormes quinquets projetant leurs lueurs
Sur des fronts ténébreux de poëtes illustres
Qui viennent gaspiller leurs sanglantes sueurs;

Voilà le noir tableau qu'en un rêve nocturne
Je vis se dérouler sous mon œil clairvoyant.
Moi-même, dans un coin de l'antre taciturne,
Je me vis accoudé, froid, muet, enviant,

Enviant de ces gens la passion tenace,
De ces vieilles putains la funèbre gaieté,
Et tous gaillardement trafiquant à ma face,
L'un de son vieil honneur, l'autre de sa beauté !

Et mon cœur s'effraya d'envier maint pauvre homme
Courant avec ferveur à l'abîme béant,
Et qui, soûl de son sang, préférerait en somme
La douleur à la mort et l'enfer au néant !

THE GAMING TABLE

On tarnished chairs the pale old harlots quiver,
Sly fatal eyes under the eyebrows painted
Dreadfully mincing : as their lean ears shiver
With hateful jewelled peal the air is tainted.

Round the green tables a frieze of lipless faces,
Of blue-cold lips, if lips, of toothless gums,
And fingers, fevered with Hell's last disgraces,
Fumbling in pockets — or in deliriums.

Dull chandeliers in the soot-mottled ceiling
And swollen lamps pick out with violet
Shadow the brows of famous poets, reeling
To waste the guerdon of art's blood-stained sweat.

My eye, turned inward, darkly can discern
This Hellish picture self distorted thus,
The while I see in yonder taciturn
Corner myself, cold, mute — and envious.

Envying these creatures their tenacious lust,
These rattling skeletons their deadly mirth,
Envying all of those who gaily thrust
Honour or beauty to rot beneath the earth.

Envious, my heart ! O dark and dreadful word !
When these with passion their bright destruction bless,
Who, drunk with the pulse of their own blood, preferred
Deep pain to death and Hell to nothingness.

— Humbert Wolfe

RÊVE PARISIEN

A Constantin Guys.

I

De ce terrible paysage,
Tel que jamais mortel n'en vit,
Ce matin encore l'image,
Vague et lointaine, me ravit.

Le sommeil est plein de miracles !
Par un caprice singulier,
J'avais banni de ces spectacles
Le végétal irrégulier,

Et, peintre fier de mon génie,
Je savourais dans mon tableau
L'enivrante monotonie
Du métal, du marbre et de l'eau.

Babel d'escaliers et d'arcades,
C'était un palais infini,
Plein de bassins et de cascades
Tombant dans l'or mat ou bruni;

Et des cataractes pesantes,
Comme des rideaux de cristal,
Se suspendaient, éblouissantes,
A des murailles de métal.

Non d'arbres, mais de colonnades
Les étangs dormants s'entouraient,
Où de gigantesques naïades,
Comme des femmes, se miraient.

PARISIAN DREAM

To Constantine Guys.

I

That marvellous landscape of my dream —
Which no eye knows, nor ever will —
At moments, wide awake, I seem
To grasp, and it excites me still.

Sleep, how miraculous you are —
A strange caprice had urged my hand
To banish, as irregular,
All vegetation from that land;

And, proud of what my art had done,
I viewed my painting, knew the great
Intoxicating monotone
Of marble, water, steel and slate.

Staircases and arcades there were
In a long labyrinth, which led
To a vast palace; fountains there
Were gushing gold, and gushing lead.

And many a heavy cataract
Hung like a curtain, — did not fall,
As water does, but hung, compact,
Crystal, on many a metal wall.

Tall nymphs with Titan breasts and knees
Gazed at their images unblurred,
Where groves of colonnades, not trees,
Fringed a deep pool where nothing stirred.

Des nappes d'eau s'épanchaient, bleues,
Entre des quais roses et verts,
Pendant des millions de lieues,
Vers les confins de l'univers;

C'étaient des pierres inouïes
Et des flots magiques; c'étaient
D'immenses glaces éblouies
Par tout ce qu'elles reflétaient !

Insouciants et taciturnes,
Des Ganges, dans le firmament,
Versaient le trésor de leurs urnes
Dans des gouffres de diamant.

Architecte de mes féeries,
Je faisais, à ma volonté,
Sous un tunnel de pierreries
Passer un océan dompté;

Et tout, même la couleur noire,
Semblait fourbi, clair, irisé;
Le liquide enchâssait sa gloire
Dans le rayon cristallisé.

Nul astre d'ailleurs, nuls vestiges
De soleil, même au bas du ciel,
Pour illuminer ces prodiges,
Qui brillaient d'un feu personnel !

Et sur ces mouvantes merveilles
Planait (terrible nouveauté !
Tout pour l'œil, rien pour les oreilles !)
Un silence d'éternité.

Blue sheets of water, left and right,
Spread between quays of rose and green,
To the world's end and out of sight,
And still expanded, though unseen.

Enchanted rivers, those — with jade
And jasper were their banks bedecked;
Enormous mirrors, dazzled, made
Dizzy by all they did reflect.

And many a Ganges, taciturn
And heedless, in the vaulted air,
Poured out the treasure of its urn
Into a gulf of diamond there.

As architect, it tempted me
To tame the ocean at its source;
And this I did, — I made the sea
Under a jeweled culvert course.

And every colour, even black,
Became prismatic, polished, bright;
The liquid gave its glory back
Mounted in iridescent light.

There was no moon, there was no sun, —
For why should sun and moon conspire
To light such prodigies ? — each one
Blazed with its own essential fire !

A silence like eternity
Prevailed, there was no sound to hear;
These marvels all were for the eye,
And there was nothing for the ear.

II

En rouvrant mes yeux pleins de flamme
J'ai vu l'horreur de mon taudis,
Et senti, rentrant dans mon âme,
La pointe des soucis maudits;

La pendule aux accents funèbres
Sonnait brutalement midi,
Et le ciel versait des ténèbres
Sur le triste monde engourdi.

LE CRÉPUSCULE DU MATIN

La diane chantait dans les cours des casernes,
Et le vent du matin soufflait sur les lanternes.

C'était l'heure où l'essaim des rêves malfaisants
Tord sur leurs oreillers les bruns adolescents;
Où, comme un œil sanglant qui palpite et qui bouge,
La lampe sur le jour fait une tache rouge;
Où l'âme, sous le poids du corps revêche et lourd,
Imite les combats de la lampe et du jour.
Comme un visage en pleurs que les brises essuient,
L'air est plein du frisson des choses qui s'enfuient,
Et l'homme est las d'écrire et la femme d'aimer.

Les maisons çà et là commençaient à fumer.
Les femmes de plaisir, la paupière livide,

II

I woke; my mind was bright with flame;
I saw the cheap and sordid hole
I live in, and my cares all came
Burrowing back into my soul.

Brutally the twelve strokes of noon
Against my naked ear were hurled;
And a grey sky was drizzling down
Upon this sad, lethargic world.

— Edna St. Vincent Millay

MORNING TWILIGHT

Reveille rang thinly from across a barrack square,
And a breath of morning troubled the street-lamps' stare.

It was that hour of the night when guilty dreams
Rise from brown, restless adolescents in swarms,
When, quaking and cringing like a blood-shot eye,
The lamp stains the coming day with its dye;
When under the body's reluctant, stubborn weight
The soul, like the lamp, renews its unequal fight;
When the air shivers as if to escape, to efface
Itself in furtive breezes drying a tear-stung face;
When woman is sick of love, as the writer of his work.

Here and there a house sent up a thin smoke.
Women of the streets, sunk in stupid sleep,

Bouche ouverte, dormaient de leur sommeil stupide;
Les pauvresses, traînant leurs seins maigres et froids,
Soufflaient sur leurs tisons et soufflaient sur leurs doigts.

C'était l'heure où parmi le froid et la lésine
S'aggravent les douleurs des femmes en gésine;
Comme un sanglot coupé par un sang écumeux
Le chant du coq au loin déchirait l'air brumeux;
Une mer de brouillards baignait les édifices,
Et les agonisants dans le fond des hospices
Poussaient leur dernier râle en hoquets inégaux.
Les débauchés rentraient, brisés par leurs travaux.

L'aurore grelottante en robe rose et verte
S'avançait lentement sur la Seine déserte,
Et le sombre Paris, en se frottant les yeux,
Empoignait ses outils, vieillard laborieux.

UNE MARTYRE

DESSIN D'UN MAITRE INCONNU

Au milieu des flacons, des étoffes lamées
  Et des meubles voluptueux,
Des marbres, des tableaux, des robes parfumées
  Qui traînent à plis somptueux,

Dans une chambre tiède où, comme en une serre,
  L'air est dangereux et fatal,
Où des bouquets mourants dans leurs cercueils de
  Exhalent leur soupir final,   [verre

Seemed all raw eyelid, and gasping lip.
— And the poor's womenfolk, hugging the chilly droop
Of lank breasts, blew on their fingers, and their soup.
The extra pinch of cold, amid that of penury,
Added, for women in labour, its insult to injury.
Slitting the fogged air, the cry of a distant cock
Broke like a jet of blood through the spasm of a cough.
Buildings still swam in vague tides of mist;
And in silenced hospitals, with a last
Convulsive rattle, the dying gave up breath,
— While night revellers staggered home, tired to death.

Morning, shivering in her robe of rose and green,
Made her hesitant way along the deserted Seine,
While Paris, rubbing tired eyes in its dark,
Woke like an ancient drudge to another day's work.

— David Paul

THE MARTYR

(*Drawing by an unknown Master*)

Amongst gilt fabrics, flasks of scent and wine,
Rich furniture, white marble, precious moulds,
Fine paintings, and rich, perfumed robes that shine
Swirled into sumptuous folds,

In a warm room, that like a hothouse stifles
With dangerous and fatal breath, where lie
Pale flowers in crystal tombs, exquisite trifles,
Exhaling their last sigh —

109

Un cadavre sans tête épanche, comme un fleuve,
Sur l'oreiller désaltéré
Un sang rouge et vivant, dont la toile s'abreuve
Avec l'avidité d'un pré.

Semblable aux visions pâles qu'enfante l'ombre
Et qui nous enchaînent les yeux,
La tête, avec l'amas de sa crinière sombre
Et de ses bijoux précieux,

Sur la table de nuit, comme une renoncule,
Repose; et, vide de pensers,
Un regard vague et blanc comme le crépuscule
S'échappe des yeux révulsés.

Sur le lit, le tronc nu sans scrupules étale
Dans le plus complet abandon
La secrète splendeur et la beauté fatale
Dont la nature lui fit don;

Un bas rosâtre, orné de coins d'or, à la jambe,
Comme un souvenir est resté;
La jarretière, ainsi qu'un œil secret qui flambe,
Darde un regard diamanté.

Le singulier aspect de cette solitude
Et d'un grand portrait langoureux,
Aux yeux provocateurs comme son attitude,
Révèle un amour ténébreux,

Une coupable joie et des fêtes étranges
Pleines de baisers infernaux,
Dont se réjouissait l'essaim de mauvais anges
Nageant dans les plis des rideaux;

A headless corpse, cascading in a flood
Hot, living blood, that soaks, with crimson stain
A pillow slaked and sated as the mud
Of a wet field with rain.

Like those pale visions which the gloom aborts
Which fix us in a still, hypnotic stare,
The head, tricked out with gems of various sorts,
In its huge mass of hair,

Like a ranunculus beside the bed,
Rests on the table, empty of all thought.
From eyes revulsed, like twilight, seems to spread
A gaze that looks at naught.

Upon the bed the carcase, unabashed,
Shows, in complete abandon, without shift,
The secret splendour that, in life, it flashed
Superbly, Nature's gift.

A rosy stocking, freaked with clocks of gold,
Clings to one leg : a souvenir, it seems :
The garter, from twin diamonds, with the cold
Stare of a viper gleams.

The singular effect of solitude
And of a languorous portrait, with its eyes
Provocative as is its attitude,
Dark loves would advertise —

And guilty joys, with feasts of strange delight,
Full of infernal kisses, omens certain
To please the gloating angels of the Night
Who swim behind each curtain.

III

Et cependant, à voir la maigreur élégante
De l'épaule au contour heurté,
La hanche un peu pointue et la taille fringante
Ainsi qu'un reptile irrité,

Elle est bien jeune encor ! — Son âme exaspérée
Et ses sens par l'ennui mordus
S'étaient-ils entr'ouverts à la meute altérée
Des désirs errants et perdus ?

L'homme vindicatif que tu n'as pu, vivante,
Malgré tant d'amour, assouvir,
Combla-t-il sur ta chair inerte et complaisante
L'immensité de son désir ?

Réponds, cadavre impur ! et par tes tresses roides
Te soulevant d'un bras fiévreux,
Dis-moi, tête effrayante, a-t-il sur tes dents froides
Collé les suprêmes adieux ?

— Loin du monde railleur, loin de la foule impure,
Loin des magistrats curieux,
Dors en paix, dors en paix, étrange créature,
Dans ton tombeau mystérieux;

Ton époux court le monde, et ta forme immortelle
Veille près de lui quand il dort;
Autant que toi sans doute il te sera fidèle,
Et constant jusques à la mort.

And yet to see her nimble strength, the risky
Swerve of the rounded shoulder, and its rake,
The tented haunch, the figure lithe and frisky,
Flexed like an angry snake,

You'd know that she was young. Her soul affronted,
Her senses stung with boredom — were they bayed
By packs of wandering, lost desires, and hunted,
And finally betrayed ?

The vengeful man, whose lust you could not sate,
(In spite of much love) nor quench his fire —
Did he on your dead flesh then consummate
His monstrous, last desire ? —

Answer me, corpse impure ! With fevered fist,
Grim visage, did he raise you up on high,
And, as your silver frosty teeth he kissed,
Bid you his last goodbye ?

Far from inquiring magistrates that sneer,
Far from this world of raillery and riot,
Sleep peacefully, strange creature, on your bier,
Of mystery and quiet.

Your lover roams the world. Your deathless shape
Watches his sleep and hears each indrawn breath.
No more than you can ever he escape
From constancy till death !

— Roy Campbell

FEMMES DAMNÉES

Delphine et Hippolyte

A la pâle clarté des lampes languissantes,
Sur de profonds coussins tout imprégnés d'odeur,
Hippolyte rêvait aux caresses puissantes
Qui levaient le rideau de sa jeune candeur.

Elle cherchait, d'un œil troublé par la tempête,
De sa naïveté le ciel déjà lointain,
Ainsi qu'un voyageur qui retourne la tête
Vers les horizons bleus dépassés le matin.

De ses yeux amortis les paresseuses larmes,
L'air brisé, la stupeur, la morne volupté,
Ses bras vaincus, jetés comme de vaines armes,
Tout servait, tout parait sa fragile beauté.

Étendue à ses pieds, calme et pleine de joie,
Delphine la couvait avec des yeux ardents,
Comme un animal fort qui surveille une proie,
Après l'avoir d'abord marquée avec les dents.

Beauté forte à genoux devant la beauté frêle,
Superbe, elle humait voluptueusement
Le vin de son triomphe, et s'allongeait vers elle,
Comme pour recueillir un doux remerciement.

Elle cherchait dans l'œil de sa pâle victime
Le cantique muet que chante le plaisir,

LESBIANS

(*Delphine and Hippolyta*)

The lamps had languisht and their light was pale;
On cushions deep Hippolyta reclined.
Those potent kisses that had torn the veil
From her young candour filled her dreaming mind.

With tempest-troubled eyes she sought the blue
Heaven of her innocence, how far away !
Like some sad traveller, who turns to view
The dim horizons passed at dawn of day.

Tears and the muffled light of weary eyes,
The stupor and the dull voluptuous trance,
Limp arms, like weapons dropped by one who flies —
All served her fragile beauty to enhance.

Calm at her feet and joyful, Delphine lay
And gazed at her with ardent eyes and bright,
Like some strong beast that, having mauled its prey,
Draws back to mark the imprint of its bite.

Strong and yet bowed, superbly on her knees,
She snuffed her triumph, on that frailer grace
Poring voluptuously, as though to seize
The signs of thanks upon the other's face.

Gazing, she sought in her pale victim's eye
The speechless canticle that pleasure sings,

Et cette gratitude infinie et sublime
Qui sort de la paupière ainsi qu'un long soupir.

— " Hippolyte, cher cœur, que dis-tu de ces choses ?
Comprends-tu maintenant qu'il ne faut pas offrir
L'holocauste sacré de tes premières roses
Aux souffles violents qui pourraient les flétrir ?

Mes baisers sont légers comme ces éphémères
Qui caressent le soir les grands lacs transparents,
Et ceux de ton amant creuseront leurs ornières
Comme des chariots ou des socs déchirants ;

Ils passeront sur toi comme un lourd attelage
De chevaux et de bœufs aux sabots sans pitié...
Hippolyte, ô ma sœur ! tourne donc ton visage,
Toi, mon âme et mon cœur, mon tout et ma moitié,

Tourne vers moi tes yeux pleins d'azur et d'étoiles !
Pour un de ces regards charmants, baume divin,
Des plaisirs plus obscurs je lèverai les voiles
Et je t'endormirai dans un rêve sans fin ! "

Mais Hippolyte alors, levant sa jeune tête :
— " Je ne suis point ingrate et ne me repens pas,
Ma Delphine, je souffre et je suis inquiète,
Comme après un nocturne et terrible repas.

Je sens fondre sur moi de lourdes épouvantes
Et de noirs bataillons de fantômes épars,
Qui veulent me conduire en des routes mouvantes
Qu'un horizon sanglant ferme de toutes parts.

The infinite gratitude that, like a sigh,
Mounts slowly from the spirit's deepest springs.

"Now, now you understand (for love like ours
Is proof enough) that 'twere a sin to throw
The sacred holocaust of your first flowers
To those whose breath might parch them as they blow.

Light falls my kiss, as the ephemeral wing
That scarcely stirs the shining of a lake.
What ruinous pain your lover's kiss would bring!
A plough that leaves a furrow in its wake.

Over you, like a herd of ponderous kine,
Man's love will pass and his caresses fall
Like trampling hooves. Then turn your face to mine;
Turn, oh my heart, my half of me, my all!

Turn, turn, that I may see their starry lights,
Your eyes of azure; turn. For one dear glance
I will reveal love's most obscure delights,
And you shall drowse in pleasure's endless trance."

"Not thankless, nor repentant in the least
Is your Hippolyta." She raised her head.
"But one who from some grim nocturnal feast
Returns at dawn feels less disquieted.

I bear a weight of terrors, and dark hosts
Of phantoms haunt my steps and seem to lead.
I walk, compelled, behind these beckoning ghosts
Down sliding roads and under skies that bleed.

117

Avons-nous donc commis une action étrange ?
Explique, si tu peux, mon trouble et mon effroi :
Je frissonne de peur quand tu me dis : "Mon ange !"
Et cependant je sens ma bouche aller vers toi.

Ne me regarde pas ainsi, toi, ma pensée !
Toi que j'aime à jamais, ma sœur d'élection,
Quand même tu serais une embûche dressée
Et le commencement de ma perdition ! "

Delphine, secouant sa crinière tragique,
Et comme trépignant sur le trépied de fer,
L'œil fatal, répondit d'une voix despotique :
— " Qui donc devant l'amour ose parler d'enfer ?

Maudit soit à jamais le rêveur inutile
Qui voulut le premier, dans sa stupidité,
S'éprenant d'un problème insoluble et stérile,
Aux choses de l'amour mêler l'honnêteté !

Celui qui veut unir dans un accord mystique
L'ombre avec la chaleur, la nuit avec le jour,
Ne chauffera jamais son corps paralytique
A ce rouge soleil que l'on nomme l'amour !

Va, si tu veux, chercher un fiancé stupide;
Cours offrir un cœur vierge à ses cruels baisers;
Et pleine de remords et d'horreur, et livide,
Tu me rapporteras tes seins stigmatisés...

On ne peut ici-bas contenter qu'un seul maître ! "
Mais l'enfant, épanchant une immense douleur,

118

Is ours so strange an act, so full of shame ?
Explain the terrors that disturb my bliss.
When you say, Love, I tremble at the name;
And yet my mouth is thirsty for your kiss.

Ah, look not so, dear sister, look not so !
You whom I love, even though that love should be
A snare for my undoing, even though
Loving I am lost for all eternity."

Delphine looked up, and fate was in her eye.
From the god's tripod and beneath his spell,
Shaking her tragic locks, she made reply :
" Who in love's presence dares to speak of hell ?

Thinker of useless thoughts, let him be cursed,
Who in his folly, venturing to vex
A question answerless and barren, first
With wrong and right involved the things of sex !

He who in mystical accord conjoins
Shadow with heat, dusk with the noon's high fire,
Shall never warm the palsy of his loins
At that red sun which mortals call desire.

Go, seek some lubber groom's deflowering lust;
Take him your heart and leave me here despised !
Go — and bring back, all horror and disgust,
The livid breasts man's love has stigmatized.

One may not serve two masters here below."
But the child answered : " I am torn apart,

Cria soudain : — " Je sens s'élargir dans mon être
Un abîme béant; cet abîme est mon cœur !

Brûlant comme un volcan, profond comme le vide !
Rien ne rassasiera ce monstre gémissant
Et ne rafraîchira la soif de l'Euménide
Qui, la torche à la main, le brûle jusqu'au sang.

Que nos rideaux fermés nous séparent du monde,
Et que la lassitude amène le repos !
Je veux m'anéantir dans ta gorge profonde
Et trouver sur ton sein la fraîcheur des tombeaux ! "

— Descendez, descendez, lamentables victimes,
Descendez le chemin de l'enfer éternel !
Plongez au plus profond du gouffre où tous les crimes,
Flagellés par un vent qui ne vient pas du ciel,

Bouillonnent pêle-mêle avec un bruit d'orage.
Ombres folles, courez au but de vos désirs;
Jamais vous ne pourrez assouvir votre rage,
Et votre châtiment naîtra de vos plaisirs.

Jamais un rayon frais n'éclaira vos cavernes;
Par les fentes des murs des miasmes fiévreux
Filtrent en s'enflammant ainsi que des lanternes
Et pénètrent vos corps de leurs parfums affreux.

L'âpre stérilité de votre jouissance
Altère votre soif et roidit votre peau,
Et le vent furibond de la concupiscence
Fait claquer votre chair ainsi qu'un vieux drapeau.

I feel my inmost being rent, as though
A gulf had yawned — the gulf that is my heart.

Naught may this monster's desperate thirst assuage, —
As fire 'tis hot, as space itself profound —
Naught stay the Fury from her quenchless rage,
Who with her torch explores its bleeding wound.

Curtain the world away and let us try
If lassitude will bring the boon of rest.
In your deep bosom I would sink and die,
Would find the grave's fresh coolness on your breast. "

Hence, lamentable victims, get you hence !
Hells yawn beneath, your road is straight and steep.
Where all the crimes receive their recompense
Wind-whipped and seething in the lowest deep

With a huge roaring as of storms and fires,
Go down, mad phantoms, doomed to seek in vain
The ne'er-won goal of unassuaged desires,
And in your pleasures find eternal pain !

Sunless your caverns are; the fever damps
That filter in through every crannied vent
Break out with marsh-fire into sudden lamps
And steep your bodies with their frightful scent.

The barrenness of pleasures harsh and stale
Makes mad your thirst and parches up your skin;
And like an old flag volleying in the gale,
Your whole flesh shudders in the blasts of sin.

Loin des peuples vivants, errantes condamnées,
A travers les déserts courez comme les loups;
Faites votre destin, âmes désordonnées,
Et fuyez l'infini que vous portez en vous !

ALLÉGORIE

C'est une femme belle et de riche encolure,
Qui laisse dans son vin traîner sa chevelure.
Les griffes de l'amour, les poisons du tripot,
Tout glisse et tout s'émousse au granit de sa peau.
Elle rit à la Mort et nargue la Débauche,
Ces monstres dont la main, qui toujours gratte et fauche,
Dans ses jeux destructeurs a pourtant respecté
De ce corps ferme et droit la rude majesté.
Elle marche en déesse et repose en sultane;
Elle a dans le plaisir la foi mahométane,
Et dans ses bras ouverts, que remplissent ses seins,
Elle appelle des yeux la race des humains.
Elle croit, elle sait, cette vierge inféconde
Et pourtant nécessaire à la marche du monde,
Que la beauté du corps est un sublime don
Qui de toute infamie arrache le pardon.
Elle ignore l'Enfer comme le Purgatoire,
Et quand l'heure viendra d'entrer dans la Nuit noire,
Elle regardera la face de la Mort,
Ainsi qu'un nouveau-né, — sans haine et sans remord.

Far from your kind, outlawed and reprobate,
Go, prowl like wolves through desert worlds apart !
Disordered souls, fashion your own dark fate,
And flee the god you carry in your heart.

— Aldous Huxley

AN ALLEGORY

Here is a woman, richly clad and fair,
Who in her wine dips her long, heavy hair;
Love's claws, and that sharp poison which is sin,
Are dulled against the granite of her skin.
Death she defies, Debauch she smiles upon,
For their sharp scythe-like talons every one
Pass by her in their all-destructive play;
Leaving her beauty till a later day.
Goddess she walks; sultana in her leisure;
She has Mohammed's faith that heaven is pleasure,
And bids all men forget the world's alarms
Upon her breast, between her open arms.
She knows, and she believes, this sterile maid
Without whom the world's onward dream would fade,
That bodily beauty is the supreme gift
Which may from every sin the terror lift.
Hell she ignores, and Purgatory defies;
And when black Night shall roll before her eyes,
She will look straight in Death's grim face forlorn,
Without remorse or hate — as one newborn.

—F. P. Sturm

ABEL ET CAÏN

I

Race d'Abel, dors, bois et mange;
Dieu te sourit complaisamment.

Race de Caïn, dans la fange
Rampe et meurs misérablement.

Race d'Abel, ton sacrifice
Flatte le nez du Séraphin !

Race de Caïn, ton supplice
Aura-t-il jamais une fin ?

Race d'Abel, vois tes semailles
Et ton bétail venir à bien;

Race de Caïn, tes entrailles
Hurlent la faim comme un vieux chien.

Race d'Abel, chauffe ton ventre
A ton foyer patriarcal;

Race de Caïn, dans ton antre
Tremble de froid, pauvre chacal !

Race d'Abel, aime et pullule !
Ton or fait aussi des petits.

ABEL AND CAIN

I

Race of Abel, eat, sleep and drink;
God smiles on you approvingly.

Race of Cain, in filth and stink
Grovel and die, miserably.

Race of Abel, your offering
Flatters the angelic nose !

Race of Cain, what time will bring
The end of your torment and woes ?

Race of Abel, your seeds take root,
And see how all your cattle prosper;

Race of Cain, within your gut
Howls hunger like an ancient cur.

Race of Abel, your innards take
Warmth from the patriarchal hearth;

Race of Cain, poor jackal, shake
With cold, crouched in the hollowed earth !

Race of Abel, make love and spawn !
Your gold spawns also in its right.

Race de Caïn, cœur qui brûle,
Prends garde à ces grands appétits.

Race d'Abel, tu crois et broutes
Comme les punaises des bois !

Race de Caïn, sur les routes
Traîne ta famille aux abois.

II

Ah ! race d'Abel, ta charogne
Engraissera le sol fumant !

Race de Caïn, ta besogne
N'est pas faite suffisamment;

Race d'Abel, voici ta honte :
Le fer est vaincu par l'épieu !

Race de Caïn, au ciel monte
Et sur la terre jette Dieu !

LES LITANIES DE SATAN

O toi, le plus savant et le plus beau des Anges,
Dieu trahi par le sort et privé de louanges,

O Satan, prends pitié de ma longue misère !

Race of Cain, you hearts that burn,
Beware of such great appetite.

Race of Abel, you browse and breed
As wanton as an orchard pest.

Race of Cain, along the roadside
Drag your family, hard pressed.

II

Ah ! race of Abel, your fat carcass
Will enrich the reeking soil !

Race of Cain, your hard work is
Not finished yet in spite of all;

Race of Abel, here your shame lies :
The sword lost to the hunter's rod !

Race of Cain, mount to the skies
And down upon the earth cast God !

— Kenneth O. Hanson

LITANY TO SATAN

O grandest of the Angels, and most wise,
O fallen God, fate-driven from the skies,

Satan, at last take pity on our pain.

O Prince de l'exil, à qui l'on a fait tort,
Et qui, vaincu, toujours te redresses plus fort,

O Satan, prends pitié de ma longue misère !

Toi qui sais tout, grand roi des choses souterraines,
Guérisseur familier des angoisses humaines,

O Satan, prends pitié de ma longue misère !

Toi qui, même aux lépreux, aux parias maudits,
Enseignes par l'amour le goût du Paradis,

O Satan, prends pitié de ma longue misère !

O toi qui de la Mort, ta vieille et forte amante,
Engendras l'Espérance, — une folle charmante !

O Satan, prends pitié de ma longue misère !

Toi qui fais au proscrit ce regard calme et haut
Qui damne tout un peuple autour d'un échafaud,

O Satan, prends pitié de ma longue misère !

Toi qui sais en quels coins des terres envieuses
Le Dieu jaloux cacha les pierres précieuses,

O Satan, prends pitié de ma longue misère !

Toi dont l'œil clair connaît les profonds arsenaux
Où dort enseveli le peuple des métaux,

O Satan, prends pitié de ma longue misère !

O first of exiles who endurest wrong,
Yet growest, in thy hatred, still more strong,

Satan, at last take pity on our pain !

O subterranean King, omniscient,
Healer of man's immortal discontent,

Satan, at last take pity on our pain.

To lepers and to outcasts thou dost show
That Passion is the Paradise below.

Satan, at last take pity on our pain.

Thou, by thy mistress Death, hast given to man
Hope, the imperishable courtesan.

Satan, at last take pity on our pain.

Thou givest to the Guilty their calm mien
Which damns the crowd around the guillotine.

Satan, at last take pity on our pain.

Thou knowest the corners of the jealous Earth
Where God has hidden jewels of great worth.

Satan, at last take pity on our pain.

Thou stretchest forth a saving hand to keep
Such men as roam upon the roofs in sleep.

Satan, at last take pity on our pain.

Toi dont la large main cache les précipices
Au somnambule errant au bord des édifices,

O Satan, prends pitié de ma longue misère !

Toi qui, magiquement, assouplis les vieux os
De l'ivrogne attardé foulé par les chevaux,

O Satan, prends pitié de ma longue misère !

Toi qui, pour consoler l'homme frêle qui souffre,
Nous appris à mêler le salpêtre et le soufre,

O Satan, prends pitié de ma longue misère !

Toi qui poses ta marque, ô complice subtil,
Sur le front du Crésus impitoyable et vil,

O Satan, prends pitié de ma longue misère !

Toi qui mets dans les yeux et dans le cœur des filles
Le culte de la plaie et l'amour des guenilles,

O Satan, prends pitié de ma longue misère !

Bâton des exilés, lampe des inventeurs,
Confesseur des pendus et des conspirateurs,

O Satan, prends pitié de ma longue misère !

Père adoptif de ceux qu'en sa noire colère
Du paradis terrestre a chassés Dieu le Père,

O Satan, prends pitié de ma longue misère !

Thy power can make the halting Drunkard's feet
Avoid the peril of the surging street.

Satan, at last take pity on our pain.

   *

Thou, to console our helplessness, didst plot
The cunning use of powder and of shot.

Satan, at last take pity on our pain.

Thy awful name is written as with pitch
On the unrelenting foreheads of the rich.

Satan, at last take pity on our pain.

In strange and hidden places thou dost move
Where women cry for torture in their love.

Satan, at last take pity on our pain.

   *

Father of those whom God's tempestuous ire
Has flung from Paradise with sword and fire,

Satan, at last take pity on our pain.

131

*The translator chose to omit these stanzas

PRIÈRE

Gloire et louange à toi, Satan, dans les hauteurs
Du Ciel, où tu régnas, et dans les profondeurs
De l'Enfer, où, vaincu, tu rêves en silence !
Fais que mon âme un jour, sous l'Arbre de Science,
Près de toi se repose, à l'heure où sur ton front
Comme un Temple nouveau ses rameaux s'épandront !.

LE VOYAGE

A Maxime du Camp.

I

Pour l'enfant, amoureux de cartes et d'estampes,
L'univers est égal à son vaste appétit.
Ah ! que le monde est grand à la clarté des lampes !
Aux yeux du souvenir que le monde est petit !

Un matin nous partons, le cerveau plein de flamme,
Le cœur gros de rancune et de désirs amers,
Et nous allons, suivant le rhythme de la lame,
Berçant notre infini sur le fini des mers :

Les uns, joyeux de fuir une patrie infâme;
D'autres, l'horreur de leurs berceaux, et quelques-uns,
Astrologues noyés dans les yeux d'une femme,
La Circé tyrannique aux dangereux parfums.

PRAYER

Satan, to thee be praise upon the Height
Where thou wast king of old, and in the night
Of Hell, where thou dost dream on silently.
Grant that one day beneath the Knowledge-tree,
When it shoots forth to grace thy royal brow,
My soul may sit, that cries upon thee now.

— James Elroy Flecker

THE VOYAGE

To Maxime du Camp.

I

For children crazed with maps and prints and stamps —
The universe can sate their appetite.
How vast the world is by the light of lamps,.
But in the eyes of memory how slight!

One morning we set sail, with brains on fire,
And hearts swelled up with rancorous emotion,
Balancing, to the rhythm of its lyre,
Our infinite upon the finite ocean.

Some wish to leave their venal native skies,
Some flee their birthplace, others change their ways,
Astrologers who've drowned in Beauty's eyes,
Tyrannic Circe with the scent that slays.

Pour n'être pas changés en bêtes, ils s'enivrent
D'espace et de lumière et de cieux embrasés ;
La glace qui les mord, les soleils qui les cuivrent,
Effacent lentement la marque des baisers.

Mais les vrais voyageurs sont ceux-là seuls qui partent
Pour partir ; cœurs légers, semblables aux ballons,
De leur fatalité jamais ils ne s'écartent,
Et, sans savoir pourquoi, disent toujours : Allons !

Ceux-là dont les désirs ont la forme des nues,
Et qui rêvent, ainsi qu'un conscrit le canon,
De vastes voluptés, changeantes, inconnues,
Et dont l'esprit humain n'a jamais su le nom !

II

Nous imitons, horreur ! la toupie et la boule
Dans leur valse et leurs bonds ; même dans nos sommeils
La Curiosité nous tourmente et nous roule,
Comme un Ange cruel qui fouette des soleils.

Singulière fortune où le but se déplace,
Et, n'étant nulle part, peut être n'importe où !
Où l'Homme, dont jamais l'espérance n'est lasse,
Pour trouver le repos court toujours comme un fou !

Notre âme est un trois-mâts cherchant son Icarie ;
Une voix retentit sur le pont : " Ouvre l'œil ! "
Une voix de la hune, ardente et folle, crie :
" Amour... gloire... bonheur ! " Enfer ! c'est un écueil !

Not to be changed to beasts, they have their fling
With space, and splendour, and the burning sky,
The suns that bronze them and the frosts that sting
Efface the mark of kisses by and by.

But the true travellers are those who go
Only to get away : hearts like balloons
Unballasted, with their own fate aglow,
Who know not why they fly with the monsoons :

Those whose desires are in the shape of clouds,
Who dream, as raw recruits of shot and shell,
Of mighty raptures in strange, transient crowds
Of which no human soul the name can tell.

II

Horror ! We imitate the top and bowl
In swerve and bias. Through our sleep it runs.
It's Curiosity that makes us roll,
As the fierce Angel whips the whirling suns.

Singular game ! where the goal changes places;
The winning-post is nowhere, yet all round;
Where Man tires not of the mad hope he races
Thinking, some day, that respite will be found.

Our soul's like a three-master, where one hears
A voice that from the bridge would warn all hands.
Another from the foretop madly cheers
"Love, joy, and glory " . . . Hell ! we're on the sands !

135

Chaque îlot signalé par l'homme de vigie
Est un Eldorado promis par le Destin;
L'Imagination qui dresse son orgie
Ne trouve qu'un récif aux clartés du matin.

O le pauvre amoureux des pays chimériques !
Faut-il le mettre aux fers, le jeter à la mer,
Ce matelot ivrogne, inventeur d'Amériques
Dont le mirage rend le gouffre plus amer ?

Tel le vieux vagabond, piétinant dans la boue,
Rêve, le nez en l'air, de brillants paradis;
Son œil ensorcelé découvre une Capoue
Partout où la chandelle illumine un taudis.

III

Étonnants voyageurs ! quelles nobles histoires
Nous lisons dans vos yeux profonds comme les mers !
Montrez-nous les écrins de vos riches mémoires,
Ces bijoux merveilleux, faits d'astres et d'éthers.

Nous voulons voyager sans vapeur et sans voile !
Faites, pour égayer l'ennui de nos prisons,
Passer sur nos esprits, tendus comme une toile,
Vos souvenirs avec leurs cadres d'horizons.

Dites, qu'avez-vous vu ?

The watchmen think each isle that heaves in view
An Eldorado, shouting their belief;
Imagination riots in the crew
Who in the morning only find a reef.

The fool that dotes on far, chimeric lands —
Put him in irons, or feed him to the shark !
The drunken sailor's visionary lands
Can only leave the bitter truth more stark.

So some old vagabond, in mud who grovels,
Dreams, nose in air, of Edens sweet to roam;
Wherever smoky wicks illumine hovels
He sees another Capua or Rome.

III

Amazing travellers, what noble stories
We read in the deep oceans of your gaze !
Show us your memory's casket, and the glories
Streaming from gems made out of stars and rays !

We, too, would roam without a sail or steam,
And to combat the boredom of our jail,
Would stretch, like canvas on our souls, a dream,
Framed in horizons, of the seas you sail.

What have you seen ?

137

IV

" Nous avons vu des astres
Et des flots; nous avons vu des sables aussi;
Et, malgré bien des chocs et d'imprévus désastres,
Nous nous sommes souvent ennuyés, comme ici.

La gloire du soleil sur la mer violette,
La gloire des cités dans le soleil couchant,
Allumaient dans nos cœurs une ardeur inquiète
De plonger dans un ciel au reflet alléchant.

Les plus riches cités, les plus grands paysages,
Jamais ne contenaient l'attrait mystérieux
De ceux que le hasard fait avec les nuages.
Et toujours le désir nous rendait soucieux !

— La jouissance ajoute au désir de la force.
Désir, vieil arbre à qui le plaisir sert d'engrais,
Cependant que grossit et durcit ton écorce,
Tes branches veulent voir le soleil de plus près !

Grandiras-tu toujours, grand arbre plus vivace
Que le cyprès ? — Pourtant nous avons, avec soin,
Cueilli quelques croquis pour votre album vorace,
Frères qui trouvez beau tout ce qui vient de loin !

Nous avons salué des idoles à trompe;
Des trônes constellés de joyaux lumineux;
Des palais ouvragés dont la féerique pompe
Serait pour vos banquiers un rêve ruineux;

IV

" We have seen stars and waves,
We have seen sands and shores and oceans too,
In spite of shocks and unexpected graves,
We have been bored, at times, the same as you.

The solar glories on the violet ocean
And those of spires that in the sunset rise,
Lit, in our hearts, a yearning, fierce emotion
To plunge into those ever-luring skies.

The richest cities and the scenes most proud
In nature, have no magic to enamour
Like those which hazard traces in the cloud
While wistful longing magnifies their glamour.

(Enjoyment adds more fuel for desire,
Old tree, to which all pleasure is manure;
As the bark hardens, so the boughs shoot higher,
And nearer to the sun would grow mature.

Tree, will you always flourish, more vivacious
Than cypress ?) None the less, these views are yours :
We took some photographs for your voracious
Album, who only care for distant shores.

We have seen idols elephantine-snouted,
And thrones with living gems bestarred and pearled,
And palaces whose riches would have routed
The dreams of all the bankers in the world.

Des costumes qui sont pour les yeux une ivresse;
Des femmes dont les dents et les ongles sont teints,
Et des jongleurs savants que le serpent caresse. "

V

Et puis, et puis encore ?

VI

" O cerveaux enfantins !
Pour ne pas oublier la chose capitale,
Nous avons vu partout, et sans l'avoir cherché,
Du haut jusques en bas de l'échelle fatale,
Le spectacle ennuyeux de l'immortel péché :

La femme, esclave vile, orgueilleuse et stupide,
Sans rire s'adorant et s'aimant sans dégoût;
L'homme, tyran goulu, paillard, dur et cupide,
Esclave de l'esclave et ruisseau dans l'égout;

Le bourreau qui jouit, le martyr qui sanglote;
La fête qu'assaisonne et parfume le sang;
Le poison du pouvoir énervant le despote,
Et le peuple amoureux du fouet abrutissant;

Plusieurs religions semblables à la nôtre,
Toutes escaladant le ciel; la Sainteté,
Comme en un lit de plume un délicat se vautre,
Dans les clous et le crin cherchant la volupté;

We have seen wonder-striking robes and dresses,
Women whose nails and teeth the betel stains
And jugglers whom the rearing snake caresses. "

v

What then ? What then ?

VI

" O childish little brains,
Not to forget the greatest wonder there —
We've seen in every country, without searching,
From top to bottom of the fatal stair
Immortal sin ubiquitously lurching :

Woman, a vile slave, proud in her stupidity,
Self-worshipping, without the least disgust :
Man, greedy, lustful, ruthless in cupidity,
Slave to a slave, and sewer to her lust :

The torturer's delight, the martyr's sobs,
The feasts where blood perfumes the giddy rout :
Power sapping its own tyrants : servile mobs
In amorous obeisance to the knout :

Some similar religions to our own,
All climbing skywards : Sanctity who treasures,
As in his downy couch some dainty drone,
In horsehair, nails, and whips, his dearest pleasures.

141

L'Humanité bavarde, ivre de son génie,
Et, folle maintenant comme elle était jadis,
Criant à Dieu, dans sa furibonde agonie :
" O mon semblable, ô mon maître, je te maudis ! "

Et les moins sots, hardis amants de la Démence,
Fuyant le grand troupeau parqué par le Destin,
Et se réfugiant dans l'opium immense !
— Tel est du globe entier l'éternel bulletin. "

VII

Amer savoir, celui qu'on tire du voyage !
Le monde, monotone et petit, aujourd'hui,
Hier, demain, toujours, nous fait voir notre image :
Une oasis d'horreur dans un désert d'ennui !

Faut-il partir ? rester ? Si tu peux rester, reste;
Pars, s'il le faut. L'un court, et l'autre se tapit
Pour tromper l'ennemi vigilant et funeste,
Le Temps ! Il est, hélas ! des coureurs sans répit,

Comme le Juif errant et comme les apôtres,
A qui rien ne suffit, ni wagon ni vaisseau,
Pour fuir ce rétiaire infâme; il en est d'autres
Qui savent le tuer sans quitter leur berceau.

Lorsque enfin il mettra le pied sur notre échine,
Nous pourrons espérer et crier : En avant !
De même qu'autrefois nous partions pour la Chine,
Les yeux fixés au large et les cheveux au vent,

Prating Humanity, with genius raving,
As mad today as ever from the first,
Cries in fierce agony, its Maker braving,
'O God, my Lord and likeness, be thou cursed!'

But those less dull, the lovers of Dementia,
Fleeing the herd which fate has safe impounded,
In opium seek for limitless adventure.
— That's all the record of the globe we rounded."

VII

It's bitter knowledge that one learns from travel.
The world so small and drab, from day to day,
The horror of our image will unravel,
A pool of dread in deserts of dismay.

Must we depart, or stay? Stay if you can.
Go if you must. One runs : another hides
To baffle Time, that fatal foe to man.
And there are runners, whom no rest betides,

Like the Apostles or the Wandering Jew,
Whom neither ship nor waggon can enable
To cheat the retiary. But not a few
Have killed him without stirring from their cradle.

But when he sets his foot upon our nape
We still can hope and cry "Leave all behind!"
As in old times to China we'd escape
With eyes turned seawards, hair that fans the wind,

143

Nous nous embarquerons sur la mer des Ténèbres
Avec le cœur joyeux d'un jeune passager.
Entendez-vous ces voix, charmantes et funèbres,
Qui chantent : " Par ici ! vous qui voulez manger

Le Lotus parfumé ! c'est ici qu'on vendange
Les fruits miraculeux dont votre cœur a faim;
Venez vous enivrer de la douceur étrange
De cette après-midi qui n'a jamais de fin ? "

A l'accent familier nous devinons le spectre;
Nos Pylades là-bas tendent leurs bras vers nous.
" Pour rafraîchir ton cœur nage vers ton Électre ! "
Dit celle dont jadis nous baisions les genoux.

VIII

O Mort, vieux capitaine, il est temps ! levons l'ancre.
Ce pays nous ennuie, ô Mort ! Appareillons !
Si le ciel et la mer sont noirs comme de l'encre,
Nos cœurs que tu connais sont remplis de rayons !

Verse-nous ton poison pour qu'il nous réconforte !
Nous voulons, tant ce feu nous brûle le cerveau,
Plonger au fond du gouffre, Enfer ou Ciel, qu'importe ?
Au fond de l'Inconnu pour trouver du *nouveau* !

We'll sail once more upon the sea of Shades
With heart like that of a young sailor beating.
I hear the rich, sad voices of the Trades
Who cry " This Way ! all you who would be eating

The scented Lotus. Here it is they range
The piles of magic fruit. O hungry friend,
Come here and swoon away into the strange
Trance of an afternoon that has no end. "

In the familiar tones we sense the spectre;
Our Pylades stretch arms across the seas.
" To salve your heart, now swim to your Electra, "
She cries, of whom we used to kiss the knees.

VIII

O Death, old Captain, it is time. Weigh anchor !
To sail beyond the doldrums of our days.
Though black as pitch the sea and sky, we hanker
For space; you know our hearts are full of rays.

Pour us your poison to revive our soul !
It cheers the burning quest that we pursue,
Careless if Hell or Heaven be our goal,
Beyond the known world to seek out the New !

— Roy Campbell

LE REBELLE

Un Ange furieux fond du ciel comme un aigle,
Du mécréant saisit à plein poing les cheveux,
Et dit, le secouant : " Tu connaîtras la règle !
(Car je suis ton bon Ange, entends-tu ?) Je le veux !

Sache qu'il faut aimer, sans faire la grimace,
Le pauvre, le méchant, le tortu, l'hébété,
Pour que tu puisses faire à Jésus, quand il passe,
Un tapis triomphal avec ta charité.

Tel est l'Amour ! Avant que ton cœur ne se blase,
A la gloire de Dieu rallume ton extase;
C'est la Volupté vraie aux durables appas ! "

Et l'Ange, châtiant autant, ma foi ! qu'il aime,
De ses poings de géant torture l'anathème;
Mais le damné répond toujours : " Je ne veux pas ! "

LE GOUFFRE

Pascal avait son gouffre, avec lui se mouvant.
— Hélas ! tout est abîme, — action, désir, rêve,
Parole ! et sur mon poil qui tout droit se relève
Maintes fois de la Peur je sens passer le vent.

En haut, en bas, partout, la profondeur, la grève,
Le silence, l'espace affreux et captivant...
Sur le fond de mes nuits Dieu de son doigt savant
Dessine un cauchemar multiforme et sans trêve.

146

THE REBEL

A furious Angel plunged from the sky like a hawk,
Gripped the sinner with rough hands by the hair,
And shaking him, shouted, "You shall obey, do you hear?
I am your Guardian Angel. No back talk!

Learn to love (for you must, and no grimaces!)
The poor, the spiteful, the deformed, the dumb;
For you must spread for Jesus when he comes
A rich carpet of Charity where he passes.

That is Love! Before your heart expire,
Let the glory of God set it afire;
That is the true Delight that cannot rot!"

Then the Angel, cruel as he was kind,
With giant hands twisted him till he whined;
But the damned soul still answered, "I will not!"

— Jackson Mathews

THE ABYSS

Pascal's abyss went with him, yawned in the air,
— Alas! All is abyss! Desire, act, dream,
Word! I have felt the wind of Terror stream
Many a time across my upright hair.

Above, below, around me, shores descending . . .
Silence . . . frightful, captivating Space . . .
At night I watch God's knowing finger trace
The dark with nightmare, multiform, unending.

147

J'ai peur du sommeil comme on a peur d'un grand trou,
Tout plein de vague horreur, menant on ne sait où;
Je ne vois qu'infini par toutes les fenêtres,

Et mon esprit, toujours du vertige hanté,
Jalouse du néant l'insensibilité.
— Ah ! ne jamais sortir des Nombres et des Êtres !

LA LUNE OFFENSÉE

O Lune qu'adoraient discrètement nos pères,
Du haut des pays bleus où, radieux sérail,
Les astres vont te suivre en pimpant attirail,
Ma vieille Cynthia, lampe de nos repaires,

Vois-tu les amoureux, sur leurs grabats prospères,
De leur bouche en dormant montrer le frais émail ?
Le poëte buter du front sur son travail ?
Ou sous les gazons secs s'accoupler les vipères ?

Sous ton domino jaune, et d'un pied clandestin,
Vas-tu, comme jadis, du soir jusqu'au matin,
Baiser d'Endymion les grâces surannées ?

— " Je vois ta mère, enfant de ce siècle appauvri,
Qui vers son miroir penche un lourd amas d'années,
Et plâtre artistement le sein qui t'a nourri ! "

Sleep itself is an enormous lair,
Filled with vague horror, leading none knows where;
All windows open upon Infinity;

My spirit, always haunted now by slumber,
Yearns for extinction, insensibility.
— Ah! never to be free of Being, Number!

— Jackson Mathews

THE MOON OFFENDED

O moon, to whom our fathers used to pray,
From your blue home, where, odalisques of light,
The stars will follow you in spruce array,
Old Cynthia, lantern of our dens by night,

Do you see sleeping lovers on their couches
Reveal the cool enamel of their teeth :
The poet at his labours, how he crouches :
And vipers — how they couple on the heath ?

In yellow domino, with stealthy paces,
Do you yet steal with clandestine embraces
To clasp Endymion's pale, millennial charm ?

— " I see your mother, by her mirror, buckled
By weight of years, poor child of death and harm !
Patching with art the breast at which you suckled ! "

— Roy Campbell

149

L'IMPRÉVU

Harpagon qui veillait son père agonisant,
Se dit, rêveur, devant ces lèvres déjà blanches :
" Nous avons au grenier un nombre suffisant,
    Ce me semble, de vieilles planches ? "

Célimène roucoule et dit : " Mon cœur est bon,
Et naturellement, Dieu m'a faite très-belle. "
— Son cœur ! cœur racorni, fumé comme un jambon,
    Recuit à la flamme éternelle !

Un gazetier fumeux, qui se croit un flambeau,
Dit au pauvre, qu'il a noyé dans les ténèbres :
" Où donc l'aperçois-tu, ce créateur du Beau,
    Ce redresseur que tu célèbres ? "

Mieux que tous, je connais certain voluptueux
Qui bâille nuit et jour, et se lamente et pleure,
Répétant, l'impuissant et le fat : " Oui, je veux
    Être vertueux, dans une heure ! "

L'Horloge à son tour, dit à voix basse : " Il est mûr,
Le damné ! J'avertis en vain la chair infecte.
L'homme est aveugle, sourd, fragile comme un mur
    Qu'habite et que ronge un insecte ! "

Et puis, quelqu'un paraît que tous avaient nié,
Et qui leur dit, railleur et fier : " Dans mon ciboire,
Vous avez, que je crois, assez communié
    A la joyeuse Messe noire ?

THE UNFORESEEN

Harpagon watched his father slowly dying
And musing on his white lips as they shrunk,
Said, " There is lumber in the outhouse lying
It seems : old boards and junk. "

Celimene cooed, and said, " How good I am
And, naturally, God made my looks excel. "
(Her callous heart, thrice-smoked like salted ham,
And cooked in the fires of Hell !)

A smoky scribbler, to himself a beacon,
Says to the wretch whom he has plunged in shade —
" Where's the Creator you so loved to speak on,
The Saviour you portrayed ? "

But best of all I know a certain rogue
Who yawns and weeps, lamenting night and day
(Impotent fathead) in the same old brogue,
" I will be good — one day ! "

The clock says in a whisper, " He is ready
The damned one, whom I warned of his disaster.
He's blind, and deaf, and like a wall unsteady,
Where termites mine the plaster. "

Then one appeared whom all of them denied
And said with mocking laughter, " To my manger
You've *all* come; to the Black Mass I provide
Not one of you's a stranger.

Chacun de vous m'a fait un temple dans son cœur;
Vous avez, en secret, baisé ma fesse immonde !
Reconnaissez Satan à son rire vainqueur,
　　Énorme et laid comme le monde !

Avez-vous donc pu croire, hypocrites surpris,
Qu'on se moque du maître, et qu'avec lui l'on triche,
Et qu'il soit naturel de recevoir deux prix,
　　D'aller au Ciel et d'être riche ?

Il faut que le gibier paye le vieux chasseur
Qui se morfond longtemps à l'affût de la proie.
Je vais vous emporter à travers l'épaisseur,
　　Compagnons de ma triste joie,

A travers l'épaisseur de la terre et du roc,
A travers les amas confus de votre cendre,
Dans un palais aussi grand que moi, d'un seul bloc
　　Et qui n'est pas de pierre tendre;

Car il est fait avec l'universel Péché,
Et contient mon orgueil, ma douleur et ma gloire ! "
— Cependant, tout en haut de l'univers juché,
　　Un ange sonne la victoire

De ceux dont le cœur dit : " Que béni soit son fouet,
Seigneur ! que la Douleur, ô Père, soit bénie !
Mon âme dans tes mains n'est pas un vain jouet,
　　Et ta prudence est infinie. "

You've built me temples in your hearts of sin.
You've kissed my buttocks in your secret mirth.
Know me for Satan by this conquering grin,
As monstrous as the Earth.

D'you think, poor hypocrites surprised red-handed,
That you can trick your lord without a hitch;
And that by guile two prizes can be landed —
Heaven, and being rich ?

The wages of the huntsman is his quarry,
Which pays him for the chill he gets while stalking.
Companions of my revels grim and sorry
I am going to take you walking,

Down through the denseness of the soil and rock,
Down through the dust and ash you leave behind,
Into a palace, built in one solid block,
Of stone that is not kind :

For it is built of Universal Sin
And holds of me all that is proud and glorious. "
— Meanwhile an angel, far above the din,
Sends forth a peal victorious

For all whose hearts can say, " I bless thy rod;
And blessèd be the griefs that on us fall.
My soul is not a toy, Eternal God,
Thy wisdom's all in all ! "

Le son de la trompette est si délicieux,
Dans ces soirs solennels de célestes vendanges,
Qu'il s'infiltre comme une extase dans tous ceux
Dont elle chante les louanges.

RECUEILLEMENT

Sois sage, ô ma Douleur, et tiens-toi plus tranquille.
Tu réclamais le Soir; il descend; le voici :
Une atmosphère obscure enveloppe la ville,
Aux uns portant la paix, aux autres le souci.

Pendant que des mortels la multitude vile,
Sous le fouet du Plaisir, ce bourreau sans merci,
Va cueillir des remords dans la fête servile,
Ma Douleur, donne-moi la main; viens par ici,

Loin d'eux. Vois se pencher les défuntes Années,
Sur les balcons du ciel, en robes surannées;
Surgir du fond des eaux le Regret souriant;

Le Soleil moribond s'endormir sous une arche,
Et, comme un long linceul traînant à l'Orient,
Entends, ma chère, entends la douce Nuit qui marche.

And so deliciously that trumpet blows
On evenings of celestial harvestings,
It makes a rapture in the hearts of those
Whose love and praise it sings.

— Roy Campbell

MEDITATION

Be tranquil, O my Sorrow, and be wise.
The Evening comes, is here, for which you sought :
The Dusk, wrapping the city in disguise,
Care unto some, to others peace has brought.

Now while the sordid multitude with shame
Obeying Pleasure's whip and merciless sway,
Go gathering remorse in servile game,
Give me your hand, my Sorrow, come this way,

Far from them. See the years in ancient dress
Along the balconies of heaven press,
Smiling Regret from deepest waters rise;

Beneath an arch the old Sun goes to bed,
And like a winding-sheet across the skies,
Hear, my Beloved, hear the sweet Night tread.

— Barbara Gibbs

MADRIGAL TRISTE

I

Que m'importe que tu sois sage ?
Sois belle ! et sois triste ! Les pleurs
Ajoutent un charme au visage,
Comme le fleuve au paysage ;
L'orage rajeunit les fleurs.

Je t'aime surtout quand la joie
S'enfuit de ton front terrassé ;
Quand ton cœur dans l'horreur se noie ;
Quand sur ton présent se déploie
Le nuage affreux du passé.

Je t'aime quand ton grand œil verse
Une eau chaude comme le sang ;
Quand, malgré ma main qui te berce,
Ton angoisse, trop lourde, perce
Comme un râle d'agonisant.

J'aspire, volupté divine !
Hymne profond, délicieux !
Tous les sanglots de ta poitrine,
Et crois que ton cœur s'illumine
Des perles que versent tes yeux !

A MADRIGAL OF SORROW

I

What do I care though you be wise ?
Be sad, be beautiful; your tears
But add one more charm to your eyes,
As streams to valleys where they rise;
And fairer every flower appears

After the storm. I love you most
When joy has fled your brow downcast;
When your heart is in horror lost,
And over your present like a ghost
Floats the dark shadow of the past.

I love you when the teardrop flows,
Hot as blood, from your large eye;
When I would hush you to repose
Your heavy pain breaks forth and grows
Into a loud and tortured cry.

And then, voluptuousness divine !
Delicious ritual and profound !
I drink in every sob like wine,
And dream that in your deep heart shine
The pearls wherein your eyes were drowned.

II

Je sais que ton cœur, qui regorge
De vieux amours déracinés,
Flamboie encor comme une forge,
Et que tu couves sous ta gorge
Un peu de l'orgueil des damnés ;

Mais tant, ma chère, que tes rêves
N'auront pas reflété l'Enfer,
Et qu'en un cauchemar sans trêves, .
Songeant de poisons et de glaives,
Éprise de poudre et de fer,

N'ouvrant à chacun qu'avec crainte,
Déchiffrant le malheur partout,
Te convulsant quand l'heure tinte,
Tu n'auras pas senti l'étreinte
De l'irrésistible Dégoût,

Tu ne pourras, esclave reine
Qui ne m'aimes qu'avec effroi,
Dans l'horreur de la nuit malsaine
Me dire, l'âme de cris pleine :
" Je suis ton égale, ô mon Roi ! "

II

I know your heart, which overflows
With outworn loves long cast aside,
Still like a furnace flames and glows,
And you within your breast enclose
A damned soul's unbending pride;

But till your dreams without release
Reflect the leaping flames of hell;
Till in a nightmare without cease
You dream of poison to bring peace,
And love cold steel and powder well;

And tremble at each opened door,
And feel for every man distrust,
And shudder at the striking hour —
Till then you have not felt the power
Of Irresistible Disgust.

My queen, my slave, whose love is fear,
When you awaken shuddering,
Until that awful hour be here,
You cannot say at midnight drear :
"I am your equal, O my King!"

—F. P. Sturm

LES PROMESSES D'UN VISAGE

J'aime, ô pâle beauté, tes sourcils surbaissés,
    D'où semblent couler des ténèbres;
Tes yeux, quoique très-noirs, m'inspirent des pensers
    Qui ne sont pas du tout funèbres.

Tes yeux, qui sont d'accord avec tes noirs cheveux,
    Avec ta crinière élastique,
Tes yeux, languissamment, me disent : " Si tu veux,
    Amant de la muse plastique,

Suivre l'espoir qu'en toi nous avons excité,
    Et tous les goûts que tu professes,
Tu pourras constater notre véracité
    Depuis le nombril jusqu'aux fesses;

Tu trouveras, au bout de deux beaux seins bien lourds,
    Deux larges médailles de bronze,
Et sous un ventre uni, doux comme du velours,
    Bistré comme la peau d'un bonze,

Une riche toison qui, vraiment, est la sœur
    De cette énorme chevelure,
Souple et frisée, et qui t'égale en épaisseur,
    Nuit sans étoiles, Nuit obscure ! "

WHAT A PAIR OF EYES CAN PROMISE

I love, pale one, your lifted eyebrows bridging
    Twin darknesses of flowing depth.
But however deep they are, they carry me
    Another way than that of death.

Your eyes, doubly echoing your hair's darkness
    — That leaping, running mane —
Your eyes, though languidly, instruct me : " Poet
    And connoisseur of love made plain,

If you desire fulfilment of the promise,
    The ecstasy that is your trade,
You can confirm the truth, from thigh to navel,
    Of all that we have said.

You will find my white breasts heavy
    With the weight of their rough, bronze coins,
And, under a soft as velvet, rounded belly,
    Poised between ambered loins,

A fleece, not golden, but for richness sister
    To that hair with darkness bright,
Supple and springing — and as boundless
    As a deep, starless night ! "

                    — David Paul

NOTES ON THE TRANSLATORS

ROY CAMPBELL (1901-1957)
Poet and translator, born in Durban, South Africa. His books include *The Flaming Terrapin, Adamastor, Flowering Rifle, Collected Poems;* he has translated plays, poems, and other works from Norwegian, Portuguese, French, and Spanish; the best known of these are the *Poems of St. John of the Cross* and the complete *Poems of Baudelaire* (1952). He has written a study of Federico García Lorca, and an autobiography, *Light on a Dark Horse.*

HENRY CURWEN (1845-1892)
English journalist, born in Cumberland, editor of *The Times of India* for fifteen years; wrote novels, among them *Lady Bluebeard,* "a story of modern society"; translated Baudelaire's "Study of the Life and Writings of Poe" (1877), and fifty-four of Baudelaire's poems in *Echoes from the French Poets* (1870) and *Some Translations from Charles Baudelaire, Poet and Symbolist* (1896).

GEORGE DILLON (b. 1906)
Poet and former editor of *Poetry,* Chicago; won the Pulitzer Prize for poetry, 1932. Poems: *Boy in the Wind* (1927), *The Flowering Stone* (1931). Collaborated with Edna St. Vincent Millay in translating *The Flowers of Evil* (1936).

163

JAMES ELROY FLECKER (1884-1915)
Poet, born in London, educated at Oxford and Cambridge; died young, of tuberculosis in a Swiss sanitarium at Davos. Officer in the consular service at Constantinople, Smyrna, Beirut. Works: *Collected Poems;* a novel, *The King of Alsander* (1914); and several plays, one of which, *Hassan of Bagdad and How He Came to Make the Golden Journey to Samarcand,* was produced in London in 1923-24 with a Fokine ballet and music by Delius.

BARBARA GIBBS (b. 1921)
Poet, born in Los Angeles, attended Stanford University and U.C.L.A. A book of her poems, *The Well,* was published in 1941. She is married to Francis Golffing and lives at Bennington College, Vermont.

KENNETH O. HANSON (b. 1922)
Poet, born in Idaho, educated at the University of Washington. His poems and translations have been published in *The New Yorker, Sewanee Review, Botteghe Oscure,* and other reviews. Now teaching at Reed College in Portland, Oregon.

ALDOUS HUXLEY (1894-1963)
Well known English novelist, essayist, poet; educated at Eton and Oxford; lived for many years in California. He translated Mallarmé's "Afternoon of a Faun."

DOROTHY MARTIN
Librarian at the Shakespeare Institute, Stratford-on-Avon. Born in Peebles, Scotland; married to Professor L. C. Martin. Author of *A First Book on Chaucer, A First Book on Shakespeare* (1930), and a volume of poems, *Sextette* (1928), which contains translations from Baudelaire, Nerval, Verlaine, Rimbaud, Mallarmé, and Laforgue.

JACKSON MATHEWS *(see page iii)*

EDNA ST. VINCENT MILLAY (1892-1950)
American poet, born in Rockland, Maine. Her first volume, *Renascence and Other Poems* (1917), brought her fame; she won the Pulitzer Prize for poetry in 1922. *Collected Sonnets* (1941), *Collected Lyrics* (1943). Translator, with George Dillon, of *The Flowers of Evil* (1936).

DAVID PAUL (b. 1914)
Poet, critic, and writer of fiction. Of Irish parentage, he was educated in the north of England. He has translated poems and plays of Baudelaire, Giraudoux, and Valéry. Lives in London.

GRAHAM REYNOLDS (b. 1914)
Deputy Keeper of Paintings, Victoria and Albert Museum. Educated at Cambridge. Author of *Twentieth Century Drawings* (1946), *English Portrait Miniatures* (1951), *Painters of the Victorian Scene* (1953).

LOIS SAUNDERS
Her volume of verse, *Strangers and Foreigners* (London, 1912), which included translations of Baudelaire, was signed from Queen's University, Kingston, Canada.

KARL SHAPIRO (b. 1913)
Poet, formerly taught at Johns Hopkins University; editor of *The Prairie Schooner*. Pulitzer Prize for poetry, 1945. Consultant in Poetry, Library of Congress, 1946-1947. Some of his books are: *Poems 1935, V-Letter and Other Poems* (1944), *Poems 1942-1953, Beyond Criticism* (1953), *Bourgeois Poet* (1964).

SIR JOHN SQUIRE (b. 1884)
Poet, editor of *London Mercury* 1919-1934, and former literary editor of *The New Statesman*. Among his books are: *Collected Parodies, Poems in One Volume, Shakespeare as Dramatist*. Lives in Sussex.

FRANK PEARCE STURM

One of the best translators of Baudelaire. Translated fifty of the poems and nineteen prose poems. Little seems to be known of him personally. The British Museum Catalogue lists, under his name: *An Hour of Reverie* (poems) 1905; *Poems of Charles Baudelaire* (Canterbury Poets Series) 1906; *Umbrae Silentes* (verse and prose) 1918; *The Eternal Helen* (poems) 1921.

RICHARD WILBUR (b. 1921)

Poet, born in New York City, educated at Amherst and at Harvard, where he was Junior Fellow and later Assistant Professor, 1950-1954. At the American Academy in Rome as winner of the *Prix de Rome,* 1954-1955. His volumes of verse are *The Beautiful Changes* (1947) and *Ceremony* (1950). He has made verse translations of Molière's *Le Misanthrope* and *Tartuffe.* In 1957 his *Things of This World* won the National Book and Pulitzer awards. Associate Professor of English at Wesleyan College.

YVOR WINTERS (b. 1900)

Poet and literary critic, and a distinguished member of the Department of English at Stanford University since 1928. He was awarded a National Institute of Arts and Letters grant in 1952; his *Collected Poems* appeared in the same year.

HUMBERT WOLFE, C.B., C.B.E. (1885-1940)

Educated at Oxford; entered the Civil Service in 1908, and was Deputy Secretary of the Ministry of Labour at his death. Among his more than forty books are: *Kensington Gardens* (1924), *The Unknown Goddess* (1925), *New's of the Devil* (1926), *The Uncelestial City* (1930), *Now a Stranger* (1933). The last is autobiographical. His translations include sonnets of Ronsard, selections from the Greek Anthology, and Rostand's *Cyrano de Bergerac.*

INDEX OF TRANSLATORS

New Directions Paperbooks – A Partial Listing

For complete listing request free catalog from
New Directions, 80 Eighth Avenue, New York 10011

† Bilingual

For complete listing request free catalog from
New Directions, 80 Eighth Avenue, New York 10011   † Bilingual